Make Money The SMART Way

A Teen's Guide to Being Financially Successful

Elizabeth Abols

Make Money the SMART Way
www.facebook.com/moneysmart4teens
Copyright © 2019 Elizabeth Abols

ISBN: 978-1-77277-288-3

All rights reserved. No portion of this book may be reproduced mechanically, electronically, or by any other means, including photocopying, without permission of the publisher or author except in the case of brief quotations embodied in critical articles and reviews. It is illegal to copy this book, post it to a website, or distribute it by any other means without permission from the publisher or author.

Limits of Liability and Disclaimer of Warranty
The author and publisher shall not be liable for your misuse of the enclosed material. This book is strictly for informational and educational purposes only.

Warning – Disclaimer
The purpose of this book is to educate and entertain. The author and/or publisher do not guarantee that anyone following these techniques, suggestions, tips, ideas, or strategies will become successful. The author and/or publisher shall have neither liability nor responsibility to anyone with respect to any loss or damage caused, or alleged to be caused, directly or indirectly by the information contained in this book.

Publisher
10-10-10 Publishing
Markham, ON Canada
Printed in Canada and the United States of America

FINANCIAL DISCLAIMER
This book and the accompanying website are for information and illustrative purposes only and do not purport to show actual results. It is not and should not be regarded as investment advice or as a recommendation regarding any particular security or course of action. Opinions expressed herein are only current opinions of the author, as of the date appearing in this material only and are subject to change without notice. The data is illustrational purpose only and information provided changes rapidly and some date can be out of date. Reasonable people may disagree about the opinions expressed herein. In the event that any of the assumptions used herein do not prove to be true, results are likely to vary substantially. All investments entail risks. There is no guarantee that investment strategies will achieve the desired results under all market conditions and each investor should evaluate their ability to invest for the long-term especially during periods of a market downturn. No representation is being made that any account, product, or strategy will or is likely to achieve profits, losses, or results similar to those discussed if any. This information is provided with the understanding that with respect to the material provided herein, you will make your own independent decision with respect to any course of action in connection herewith and as to whether such course of action is appropriate or proper based on your own judgment, and that you are capable of understanding and assessing the merits of a course of action. The author, publisher and accompanying website do not purport to and do not, in any fashion, provide tax, accounting, actuarial, recordkeeping, legal, broker/dealer or any related services. You may not rely on the statements contained herein. The author, publisher and accompanying website shall not have any liability for any damages of any kind whatsoever relating to this material. You should consult your advisors with respect to these areas. By accepting this material, you acknowledge, understand and accept this foregoing.

Table of Contents

Dedication	v
Foreword	vii
Chapter 1: Financial Basics	1
Chapter 2: How I Started Using the SMART Model	17
Chapter 3: Save	29
Chapter 4: Make Money	41
Chapter 5: Analyze	51
Chapter 6: Read Reviews to Check the Quality	61
Chapter 7: Track	73
Chapter 8: Avoid Temptations	85
Chapter 9: Cheap or Free Ways to Have Fun	97
Chapter 10: What You Can Do To Be Financially Successful	109
About the Author	121

*To my mom: Without her, I would not be where I am today.
She taught me from a young age how to be financially literate,
and supports me through challenges.*

*To my sister, Kathleen, and Grandma,
thank you for being there for me.*

*To my grandpa, and dad, who have passed away,
thank you for loving me.*

*To my dearest friends, Emily, Ana, and Stephanie, you are all
close to my heart. Never change who you are.*

*To Pumpkin and Felix, my past and present cats,
I will love you forever.*

Foreword

Make Money the SMART Way by Elizabeth Abols is intended to help you understand that you can be successful at saving and spending your money. It's easy to remember her techniques, thanks to the acronym that she uses. SMART stands for save, make money, analyze, research, and track it. This book will encourage and guide you through the challenges of saving money. From start to finish, this book is informative yet interesting enough to keep your attention.

Elizabeth makes sure to define unknown terminology and give detailed examples. This will help you understand basic financial terms that will help you become financially literate. You can easily relate to the author as she is a teen herself, and acknowledges challenges that you might face in your journey to successfully manage your money. She believes that it's important for you, as a teenager, to learn about how to manage your money, because the sooner you start saving, the more money you will have!

Finance is usually considered a boring topic, but Elizabeth makes sure to keep your attention by using easy to understand language, and thanks to this you will understand her! Elizabeth might not have any official degree, but the amount of knowledge she has learned throughout her life has all been noted down for you. You will learn how to use technology to your advantage. Phones aren't just for Instagram! Elizabeth includes multiple apps that can not only help you track how much you are spending, but also show you how to save money. You can tell how much passion Elizabeth has for personal finance. I can feel her excitement for the subject, and I know that you will be inspired to make significant changes to how you spend and save your money.

After reading this book, you will be inspired to take control of your situation and make that money! Learn to apply her techniques in the real world, and see how much you will mature and bloom into a knowledgeable adult! I hope this book will inspire you to do something you've never thought of doing. Maybe you'll start you own business, or get a job to make your own income. I just know that you'll enjoy reading this book, and I hope you can learn from it!

Raymond Aaron
New York Time Bestselling Author

Chapter 1

Financial Basics

What is Personal Financial Literacy?

Personal financial literacy is when someone is taught about essential skills and knowledge of finance. This allows the person to make an informed and educated decision on financial matters. For you, this means being able to control your spending urges, and put away money for post- secondary education, or save up for something you want. I think that everyone, not just teens, should learn about personal finance, as being financially stable and successful enhances one's life. Personal financial literacy can be split up into four parts: earnings, savings, investing, and spending. Unlike when you're an adult and you have a fulltime job, teenagers either have a part time job or no job at all. Even if you don't have a job, it's possible to earn money. How? It's simple; do chores around the house to earn money. For example, cut the grass and get $5. You could also do chores for your neighbours, and earn money.

Another way to earn money is to start your own business. This doesn't mean you have to create a massive business the way Steve Jobs, the creator of Apple, or Mark Zuckerberg from Facebook, did. You could start with selling lemonade or walking your neighbour's dog. Not only do you earn money, but you develop responsibility.

The next way to be financially literate is to learn how to save money. You know that money you got from your birthday, Bar Mitzvah, Eid, or from your grandmother? Learning how to save money means being able to distinguish what is a want and what is a need. A need is something that you need to survive in life—like water, clothing, and food—while a want is something that isn't needed to survive, and can be more materialistic. You may need a winter coat to survive a cold climate, but do you need a Canada Goose coat? This could also include things like a new Nintendo Switch, a car, or the newest smartphone. Teens have to contend with a lot of peer pressure, which can make controlling spending urges difficult. But this is part of the journey if you're going to start saving up money.

Investing money is something that can be challenging for teens to do. If you want to invest your money, then go to a financial advisor, research information from books and websites, or ask your parents. I won't be talking about investing money because I want to be focusing more on saving and spending your money.

Spending money is something that is easy to do and can be very rewarding. As soon as you buy something, you are immediately gratified with a service or product. If you don't learn how to spend money wisely, you could end up broke, with a lot of useless items.

This book will help you become knowledgeable about how to spend and save your money. By following the SMART model, you will learn how to make the most of the money you earn or are given. SMART stands for *s*ave money, *m*ake money, *a*nalyze data, and *r*esearch and *t*rack how much you earn and spend. By using this model, you'll be able to save up for big purchases, like a car and/or post-secondary education, and be on your way for a down payment on a home. But before I talk about how the smart model will improve your financial situation, I'll tell you why you want to save money in the first place.

Why Should I Save Up Money?

The answer is simple: Before purchasing items, you should have enough money saved to cover the cost. Do you plan to beg your parents for money for the rest of your life? There's a lot of teens who are spoiled. I mean really, really spoiled. I once watched a Dr. Phil episode where a girl was given an allowance of $10,000 per month when she was only 15 years old. She spent that money on designer purses, shoes, and ridiculous shopping sprees. Because she was never taught how to save money, she only knew how to spend. She reverted into a never-ending cycle of getting money and spending it. This example can be a lesson because that girl, without a serious financial intervention, is likely to have money problems throughout her life.

Some positives of saving money include learning self-control, being conscious of your decisions, and having money to spend when you need to. Saving money is also a good thing. In case something happens, it's a safety net. For example, you might have a laptop that breaks down, and you need to buy a new one for school. You will need money. Without an emergency fund, how are you going to get a new laptop? This example shows how you should think before you buy, and how important saving is so you have money for the future.

The thing about saving is that you don't get instant gratification. Instant gratification is when you do an action and you immediately feel a sense of satisfaction. For example, you see a cool looking phone case, and maybe it's cute or unique, and you want it. So, you buy it, and you feel good because you now have the case. But you have given something in return; in this case, you gave your money. Maybe it isn't even your money—you begged your parents to buy it for you. Either way, someone had to give their time and effort to get the money. Everyone needs to respect money, as it represents the time and efforts of people who have worked to get it. Teens should be grateful that their parents have worked so hard, so they can have a good life. If your family doesn't have a lot of money, this is your chance to help them, and yourself, to be successful.

What Does Success Mean for You?

Success is something that is different for each person. Some people consider being in the top one percent of wealth to be successful. Others feel that success is when you have enough money to pay your bills but be comfortable enough that you can go out every now and then for leisure activities, like seeing a movie. For teens, success may have a different definition. For a lot of teens, they're still in high school, and success could vary from getting the highest mark in the class to passing the class. Every person is different. As a student, your idea of success may just be graduating from high school and getting your diploma. For me, success in high school meant getting marks above 80 and putting all my effort into my work. In grade 12, I got the highest mark in English, with a 93. I unfortunately missed getting the highest mark in Math, by 1% (I got a 90). But I don't consider this not being successful, as I still got 10% higher than my goal.

Financial Basics

I think being successful, for teens moneywise, is when you have a part time job or some way that you're getting income. What happens if you can't get a part time job? Maybe your parents are overprotective, or maybe the places you applied to never contacted you. You can still make money other ways. You could deliver flyers, cut the neighbour's grass, or look after your friend's pet when they're on vaction. Ask neighbors if you could shovel their driveway, or ask your parents if they could pay you to do tasks for them, like cleaning the car or raking the leaves. I don't think getting an allowance from your parents without putting in some form of work is being successful. What happens when your parents stop giving you that allowance, and you're left to fend for yourself? You don't want to be living in your parent's basement when you're 30 years old, playing video games all day and mooching off their money. Of course, sometimes circumstances are out of your control, and a company went out of business, or something bad really happened in your life, like an accident and you're forced to move in.

Even though everyone has their own definition of success, I think that the main idea is that you're a productive member of society. This may seem hard for teenagers, as this is usually their first job or, for the first time, they're fending for themselves. The scariest part of becoming an adult is having to pay your own bills and live independently from your parents. I'm personally at the point where I'm attending college and able to live at home, as my community has a variety of options for post-secondary education. Thanks to this, I'm living with my mom instead of going into residence. I first thought that living in residence would make me more independent because I have to buy my own groceries, pay my rent, and also monitor how much I'm spending. Not only that, but I have to keep up with my studies. One of my fears of living with my mom during college is that I'm not going to be as independent. She would still be nagging me about certain things, and I wouldn't have to pay rent; but I do have to pay for my own food, keep the house clean, and do small day-to-day chores. This is saving me more money in the long run, so I can use that money to maybe invest in stocks or use it for my education. Because I'm living with my mom, I'm saving 10,000 plus dollars each year of my schooling. My program is 3 years long, so that's about $30,000 just for residence, without counting food expenses and other things, like heating and Wi-Fi. Instead, I have to pay for my tuition myself. My mom's not helping me at all with my tuition or for my bussing. I think this is a pretty fair deal because it is only about $5,000 a year for college and bussing. Even though it's kind of expensive, it's much cheaper than paying rent. I know, some people want to move out of their parents' house as soon as possible, or even out of the city, because they just want to have some independence, but I just want to let you know that it's okay to go to a college or university near you, and live at your house and just bus it. Who knows? Maybe in second year, you might rent a place with some friends.

Impulse Buying – What Is It?

When you do start to earn your own money, you shouldn't just spend it all immediately on an item. Impulse buying is when you buy something without thinking about how you got the money that you're about to spend (work, chores), or where it's coming from (mom, dad, etc.). Also, is the item that you're buying worth the effort you put in to gain that money. For example, I'm someone that spends most of my money on food or clothes when I go shopping. I don't really see a need for expensive jewelry or purses, or to keep up with trends, but when I'm with friends, I kind of need to eat. Whenever I go shopping, I try to think about what I really need. I'd rather spend $10 on food and not feel hungry, rather than on a cute necklace that I'll probably end up losing; but I can save even more money by eating before I leave, so I'm not hungry at all, or going home early and eating some homemade food.

I could also save more money by bringing snacks. This doesn't have to be unhealthy snacks, like chips or granola bars; you could just bring an apple. But everyone values things differently. For some of my friends, they'd rather spend their money on a really expensive pair of shoes, like Jordans, but they never end up wearing them. Instead, they just keep them in a plastic box to show off to their friends (they're limited edition, $500 shoes). Or maybe someone spends a lot of their money on makeup because they want to look good. Something that I tend to buy a lot is phone cases, and I buy a new backpack every year. I find my weakness is buying things on Amazon, so something I try to do to save money is literally to not tempt myself. If you don't see it, you don't know you "need" it.

Also, another tip that people can use is planning ahead. For example, don't go grocery shopping when you're hungry, because you'll buy more things. Just like when you get a paycheck, you shouldn't just spend everything that you just earned. Before I buy something, I always make sure that I know how many hours it is going to take to get the money back that I spent, and if I really, really want the product. Sometimes that means not picking up the product that day, and I have gained another day if I really still think about it. The problem about online shopping is that trying to return a package is really a pain in the butt; but one of the best places to buy items online is

Amazon because they provide free return postage. I personally keep some of the containers that Amazon gives me so I can just reuse them in case I have to return something that is either defaulted or broken. Some of the consequences of impulse buying are running out of money because you spent all of it, or ending up with a lot of things that you never use, and your house becomes crowded with items, making it look like a hoarder's house.

One of the most popular reasons that people impulse buy is when they become emotional. Maybe you're having a bad day at work, and you think that a cute, expensive watch will lift your moods. This will lift your mood temporarily, as it's kind of that *buyers high*, where you get endorphins that make you feel good. Another example is when you're feeling down or sad, and you want to lift your spirits by buying something. For some people, this means eating their feelings. Maybe they buy some ice cream, and this not only affects their wallet but also their health. I think that companies have really good marketing techniques that make you think that you really need their product, and that's exactly what I'm going to talk about in the next chapter.

Examples of Marketing Techniques

Marketing is when you promote a service or product to consumers (buyers), which makes someone want to buy their product. Some of the marketing techniques that companies use in a mall is making you think that if you don't get their item right now, then it will either sell out or a deal will end. That's why, when you see items in the store, the sign usually says for a limited time or until a certain date. Malls will also put a sign saying that there's a limit of a certain amount of products. They only do this

Financial Basics

to make you want to buy the max limit of the product. A deal that is really popular is the BOGO deal. Now, the BOGO deal used to be buy-one-get-one free, but a lot of stores have changed this to buy-one-get-one 50% off. This may sound like a good deal, but if you really pay attention, that's only 25% off each item. For example, if I were to buy two $10 tops, I would only get $4 off. But then, in Canada, their sales tax is 13%, which is about $2.60. So really, you're only getting about 12% off each item. Not only that, but instead of spending $10 on one top, you now spent double the amount that you intended. Another marketing strategy that stores use is fancy wording and statistics, or even fake facts. If it sounds too good, it probably is too good.

Whenever a product says that they are the number one product, or that they have a lifetime warranty, there's usually a lot of tiny conditions for that warranty. For example, if you get a certain phone that's related to a fruit, you get a one year warranty, but what you don't read is the fine conditions that are in really, really small, fine print. This includes things like water damage voiding the warranty, and you end up still paying a big sum of money to get a new phone. Now, I know that a lot of people don't read the terms and conditions because they're usually ridiculously long, and I personally don't read all the terms and conditions that I agree to; but the ones that are the most important to read are for big ticket items, like your phone, or rent or phone bill, and even return policies. Another marketing technique that stores use is an extended warranty. Now, for some people, like myself, I buy the extended warranty for my phone. I'm someone who goes through phones really fast because I'm very clumsy. I've had my phones lost, stolen, water damaged, dropped, and broken, and the extended warranty helps me save money because I can get a new phone at a largely discounted rate. But for some things, you really don't need an extended warranty, like on a TV or furniture, and definitely not for a toy. Another way that companies market specifically to teens is through social media. Whenever you're scrolling through Instagram, you see a lot of ads, but something I want to tell you about those ads, especially the ones that say *free merchandise*, is that it's a scam. How is it a scam, you ask? Simply because they make you pay for shipping, and usually the shipping is actually more than what the item is valued at.

I once got a Tamagotchi for "free." It was an impulse buy, and the shipping cost me $8. It turns out that these Tamagotchis were knockoffs, and they were valued at $2. Not only that, but I got them for months after purchasing them, and customer service does not help you at all— they won't give you a refund or tracking. A lot of the items that come from the free item are usually low quality, and they either break or, for some people, they don't even show up. I think a smart way to stop yourself from buying online is to delete your card info from your phone so it's harder for you to get to it, and it gives you that time to reflect if you really need that product. You have to go through your wallet to find the info and type it in. I feel like our generation has become really used to seeing ads everywhere, from our phones to TV commercials, to ads in the real world, on posters or cars. I know that I will always want more than what I have, but now I reflect more on what I already have and if I really need it. Thanks to this, I have been able to ask myself if I really need it or if I just want it. I'm not going to say that I have complete control over my impulse buying, because I don't. I still buy things that I regret having bought, but that's just life, and you live and learn.

Financial Basics

How to Make the Most Out of Your Money (possible investing or starting a business)

How do you think you would spend $100? Some people would just spend the whole amount on a big ticket item like a tablet or expensive makeup. But for other people, they may put away $70 and only spend 30 percent of their earnings. One of the ways that I make the most of my money is that I try to limit myself to buying or spending my money only once a week. This may be going out with friends or just buying food at a restaurant once a week, which is usually $15, or buying $25 online. But something that I have that some teens don't have is a steady income. Every two weeks, I'm paid about an average of $300. In two weeks, if I spend $50 of that $300, I am spending about 17% of my earnings while saving 83 percent in my bank account. I try to buy things that are actually useful to me, like a protective phone case so my phone doesn't break, or a necklace organizer, or retainer cleaner tablets that kill bacteria in my retainer. I try to buy less materialistic items, like clothes, in a way that I can save money. I usually don't buy my clothing full price. I go to the clearance section in a store, or I love to go to thrift stores, which usually has shirts that cost five to seven dollars instead of 15 to 25 dollar shirts, and the amount that you save adds up quickly. You might be wondering why I am saving up all this money. Maybe you want to buy a big-ticket item, like a cell phone or a laptop, or a fancy pair of Jordan sneakers. Or maybe you want to save up for college or a house.

Maybe you are a young adult, and you have to pay bills. Either way, it's good to have an amount of money saved up for emergencies. What happens if your parents lose their job and need a little bit of support from you? They have been giving you support your whole life, and it's your turn to support your family. Or maybe you face an emergency yourself: your phone breaks, and you have to buy a new one, or your data goes over the plan and you have to pay extra. Or maybe you just want to save money for when you're older. I personally started saving money when I was a little child. My mom was someone who taught me to be money smart from a young age, and thanks to this, I have saved up at least $2,000 from birthday and Christmas money. Another way to make the most of your money is to invest it. Now, for a teen, that might sound really scary, but you can research things like opening up a brokerage account or even starting with a bank account that you gain interest on every month. If you want to find more info, I don't suggest talking to the bank. The only thing they're interested in is selling you certain products because they get commission on it. If your parents aren't very money savvy, you can try asking a friend or Googling it.

Another way to invest your money is by supporting a business that you think will be successful. Or maybe you want to start your own business. But if you're not ready to invest your money, you can make the most of your money by saving it and spending it wisely. Hopefully, my introduction tips have helped you understand basic business fundamentals, like what impulse buying is and how to save and spend wisely. After reading this book, you'll become financially literate in your own personal finance. Personal financial literacy is when you're confident or knowledgeable about managing your personal financial matters, like making appropriate decisions about how to budget and invest your money, or even pay for college. In the next nine chapters, I'll be going into more detail of how I started saving my money, and sharing my tips and tricks with you, but to begin with, what does smart mean?

What Does SMART Stand For?

Smart stands for *save, make money, analyze, research, and thrift it*. I made up this acronym to help you make the right decisions when it comes to money. Hopefully, this acronym will help you in your daily life, not only when it comes to money but in normal basic decisions, like thinking before you act. Before you take a swig of that drink or a puff of that joint, you think about the consequences that may occur because of your actions. Now, this is an extreme example of how your actions and thoughts may affect you negatively. I don't mean to think that all teens are trying out drugs, but everyone makes bad decisions—you may have been spending too much money. Being able to save is a life skill that you need in order to become successful in life. If you never learn to save your money, you're not going to have any money to spend. Saving money has long-term gratification. This means that you don't get instant gratification because you didn't buy an item, but after a few months of saving up, you'd be able to buy that more expensive item that makes you feel satisfied, because you worked hard to buy that item instead of getting it immediately.

Making money is when you have a source of income, such as a job doing chores around the house for your parents, or going door-to-door asking neighbors if there's anything you could do for them to earn money, or even starting your own business. It doesn't have to be a new idea. It could be as simple as making lemonade and selling it for a dollar. Another way to make money is by selling things that you don't want, in a garage sale. Analyze means taking that moment to think before buying, and also figuring out how long it's going to take for you to pay back the amount that you spent, and if it's worth buying. Research is when you look online for cheaper prices and sales deals, or you look up reviews to see if the product is any good. I personally also search for coupons online, or promo codes that can help lower the price of your item. I think that researching is smart to do because sometimes it only takes a few minutes to save a lot of money. It may have been a promo code for free shipping, or you can even contact the store and ask them if it's possible to get free shipping. I've done this, where I didn't buy a product and they contacted me, asking why, and I just said it was too expensive, and they gave me my shipping for free. The last way that you can be smart with your money is by thrifting. Thrifting means buying things second hand at a thrift store, like Value Village. There are some really good thrift stores with brand names like Gucci, for a really big discount. Another way to thrift is by going to stores like Winners, where there are brand names for cheaper prices, or even going to a warehouse-like store, like Costco or Ikea.

I hope that my acronym, SMART, helps you with your everyday decisions, and that you share it with others. Your parents will be really impressed that you are growing up so fast and making smart decisions. Maybe you'll teach your parents a thing or two about being financially literate, and your whole family can benefit from this book. In the next chapter, I will be talking about my own personal experiences and how they've helped shape me to be the person I am today. Thanks to these experiences, I was able to create this book. I hope that this is a less formal way to talk to teens than a book written by adults, which may be too serious or factual, which is why I try to write like I'm just talking to a close friend. Just so you know, you are a close friend to me, as you've taken the initiative to read my book and make yourself a better person.

Financial Basics

Notes

Notes

Chapter 2

How I Started Using the SMART Model

My Childhood Habits

There is no age limit as to when you should start to save up money. The earlier you start saving, the better. Whenever I got money for Christmas or birthdays, I would immediately put it in my bank account. The money I would spend would be the $5 allowance my mom would give me every 2 weeks. Back in elementary school, we had something called pizza day, which would happen every Friday. It would cost $5 for a slice of pizza, a juice box, and a pack of gummies. I would not always buy this, as it would be the price of my whole allowance. I remember when I was little, if I wanted something that was more expensive, then I would have to pay for either all of it or half of it. An example of this would be when I wanted a Polly pocket toy, which cost around $20 at the time. I had to save up my money to buy it.

My grandma would sometimes reward my sister and me with toonies if we did things like clean up our room or rake the leaves. I think it's important to start teaching your kids about being financially literate from a young age. This way, they can come to appreciate money and realize how much effort is made to make it. You don't have to make the child pay for everything you buy them, but they should have to save up money that is given to them from getting good grades or doing chores. This way, they won't just play with a toy for a few minutes because that's how much time it took for them to get it. Instead, they would make good use of the object because it took them a week of saving to earn it. When I was a kid, I didn't play with toys as much as watching TV, but I did still buy some. Something that is different today is that kids don't really seem to be playing with toys; instead, they are given an iPad (which is a huge investment) that has apps to play games on.

Most apps are free, and watching cartoons is free as well. Maybe the child should have to do something to be rewarded with a tablet, like keeping their room clean for a month, or helping around the house. But as a teenager, my mom started paying for less things, and gave me the choice on how I would spend my money. For example, I might be given $20. I could use this money for when I went out to eat with friends, use it on clothing, or put it in the bank so I could buy a big ticket item. She still would pay for clothes, food, and recreational activities like swimming, but when I wanted to hang with friends, that would be my own money I'd have to use. Now that I turned 18 years old, I'm in my first year of college and am living at home to save money, as it's only a 45-minute commute. My mom pays for food, and anything to do with the house, like electricity, and I pay for my own amenities. This would include medications, toothbrush, pads, clothes, and also things that are not needed, like makeup, games, and my cat's needs, like food, kitty litter, and vet bills.

How I Started Using the SMART Model

My Mom's Influence

I don't think I would be this well off if my mom had not started teaching me about financial literacy. Back when I was really young, she made bank accounts for each of us, and professional emails. When I was a kid, I did not have a silly email like soccerlover2094@hotmail.com. No, I had an email that listed my first name and middle name, at Hotmail.ca. Having a bank account from a young age meant that I could start saving very early on. I would get birthday and Christmas money, and put it in my bank account. My mom made sure that I knew the value of money and how it should not be spent willy-nilly. Now that I'm older, my mom has taught me terms like passive income, and how houses always increase in value while cars decrease. Passive income is when you don't have to do anything and you receive money. An example of this would be if you rent out your basement: the person would be giving you money to live in your house, and you don't have to do anything. It could also be money from the government, called benefits. My mom did not just buy my sister and me what we wanted; she made sure that we had to earn the things we wanted.

When we were younger, we would be rewarded for good behaviour or marks, with stuffed animals or a game. Once we got older, we would be given money that we could either save up to buy something that was more expensive, or spend it immediately. I think that parents nowadays just buy things for their children without thinking if they did something to deserve it. Now that I'm a young adult with a job, I can decide how I want to spend the money I earn. Once you get a job, it does become more challenging because you are in control of your money. You can choose whether to spend it all or save it for when you're older. This money could be used for college or university, or for saving up for a car/housing. Every parent and guardian has their own ways of raising their children. Some parents are not financially literate themselves, so how can they teach their children?

My grandparents would always avoid questions on finance, so my mom only started to learn about money once she was older. She herself had to seek out info by reading books like the *Wealthy Barber*. The good news for you is that you've started to learn how to be financially wealthy as a teenager! Maybe you could teach your parents so they can start saving money now! Now that I'm a teenager, my mom still pays attention to what I'm buying. If she thinks I'm about to buy something unnecessary, she will tell me. Not only that, but she would also bring attention to sales and buying things used. This does require more effort, as you would have to look through the clearance section for something that is your size, and if you like the design.

Take Responsibility for Your Actions

This is something that is really important on how to start saving money. If you buy something you don't need that ends up being clutter, then you should accept that you made a mistake and not do it again. An example of something I did was buying a $300 Gucci scarf. First of all, I mostly purchased it because of its brand, but another problem with this is that I never wear the scarf, and I really should have returned it when I received it, but I didn't, and now I have a scarf that's just laying around in my room. This money was money that I wasted, and I acknowledge the mistake I made and will not be purchasing anything else

How I Started Using the SMART Model

because of its brand name. Instead, I will buy things that are not only useful to me but are worth how much it costs.

An example where I spent my money wisely would be when I bought a pair of UGG boots to replace the ones that were very worn out. It cost me $130, but I wear them almost every day, so it was money well spent. I think that is important to think before buying, but no one is perfect. There will always be impulse buys. If you do succumb to buying something in the moment, then acknowledge that you did so, but don't beat yourself up over it. If you really want it when you buy it, make sure to keep track of the receipt so you can return it. Either that or just learn from it. Something that I do when buying things is trying to reason why I'm buying something. For example, if I just finished a semester in college and got good marks, I treated myself by shopping for clothes (even though I have clothes), and I got my nails done. I think it's easy to reason why you need or deserve something, but it's even harder to reason as to why you don't need something.

Every person is different. Some people have no interest in shopping or buying things unless they absolutely need it (like my sister), while others are susceptible to wanting to buy more. For me if I see something that is cute, I am more inclined to buy it. But as my mom likes to say "Just because you want it, doesn't mean you need it". It's up to you to identify what type of spender you are. Do you spend money every single day, or only when necessary? I'm guessing that if you're reading this book, then you are someone who splurges. That isn't a bad thing though; you should be proud that you've taken the initiative to try and change your bad habits and find a way to save the money you earn or get.

**How I Use SMART
(save and make money)**

Before I tell you ways that you can be SMART, I'll first tell you how I use the SMART model when dealing with money. To begin with, let's start with the first letter of the model: **S**, which stands for *save*. Whenever I get money from work or holidays, I put it in my bank account. For work, I am paid every 2 weeks, around $320. I would then make a goal as to how much of that money I would spend. This would include things that I need, like feminine products, hygiene, and food, and then the things that I want, like new video games, clothes, and junk food. For example, if I have a goal of spending $50/week, then I would put $200 in the bank and have the rest of the money to spend. If I am given money for Christmas, I would spend 20% of it and put the rest in my bank account. Thanks to this technique, before I started having a job, I had around two thousand dollars already saved up.

Something else I did for saving money was having the actual bills so I could notice how much I physically had spent. This could be hard because I do buy a lot online, so I regularly check my bank accounts to see how much I have. Making money was something that came easy to me. When I was younger, I would do chores around the house to get money, or I would only want money for Christmas and birthdays. This is because you can choose how you want to use the money you get, versus having a present you may or might not like. Once I was done grade 10, I decided it was time to look for a job. I'll tell you now that the hardest thing to do is finding a job. Before I got the job I have, I applied to three other places. Some were online, where you had to answer questions, while others were by handing in a resume to the manager. At one store, I gave a resume, introduced myself, and never received a reply at all. Another place said they were not hiring. The one that I applied for online never contacted me at all. The final place I applied to, the day that I handed in the resume, the manager did not even read it. Instead, he asked what days I was available, and told me to come the next day to start training. In the summer after grade 11 finished, I applied for a second job.

This job had more competition; it was a group of applicants, and we had to do activities and interviews. People were then asked to leave, until 5 people were left, and this included me. After that, we were told to come next week for training. That job did pay more than my other job but required a lot more work that was unpaid, because you were only paid for the appointments you made. I would be spending two hours just taking public transit to meet the client for an appointment. This was a job where I did a demonstration of how good a product was and why they should buy it. I am really grateful for this job, as I learned a lot of marketing techniques and how to present myself to be professional. I think it is important for a teenager to start to make their own money, so they realize how much effort it takes to earn money.

Analyze and Research

Before you buy a product, it is important to research about it. This mostly applies to bigger ticket items, like headphones, a phone, or shoes. Something that I always do before purchasing headphones would be to compare multiple brands or models by looking at the features. I also compare different websites. I find that it is more difficult to compare stores, because you have to walk back and forth between the stores, and then go back to the better deal, which can sometimes be bought by someone else.

Something I do in the store is ask if they can put an item on hold for me. If they can't put the item I want on hold, then I just hide the article somewhere unexpected, like behind a blanket or inside a box. Another thing you can do, if you like to shop in an actual store, is to do research on the actual product. This can save you time because you can compare the price to other stores using your phone, or you can see what other people think about the product. I do this a lot when I buy something that I've never tried before, like shampoo. Something you can also do is analyze if you need it. You can figure out how long it will take for you to earn the money you are spending. Before I bought my phone, I made sure to do the math as to how long it would take to pay it back.

For example, my phone bill would be $50 for the plan and $15 for the phone. I would have to do that for 24 months, so $75x24=$1,800. I would then write down the price for just the phone, which would be around $930. I would then do the price of the plan by itself, and compare which was a better deal. In the end, I chose the cheaper one, which would be the two-year plan. Your math teacher is right in saying that you will use math in the *real world*, but as you can see, it's really basic math that anyone can do! Another thing you should calculate would be how long it would take to pay it off. So if I have to pay a bill of $1,800, where I'm paid $14/hour, I would divide $1,800 by 14, which is 129 hours. If I work 15 hours a week, it will take me 8.6 weeks to pay it off. This way of analyzing how long it will take to pay things off really helped me realize how much effort it would take to buy the phone, and if it is worth it.

How I Started Using the SMART Model

Thrift and Track It

The last technique that I do a lot is to *thrift it!* This means going to thrift stores or buying things second hand from apps like Kijiji. Going to thrift stores is really awesome because it has a mix of different styles, and because it is clothes from different stores, different times, and sometimes even different places. The best part is that the clothes are usually separated by size, so you just have to quickly look at the clothes in your section.

A thrift store that I recommend would be Value Village. I find that the Salvation Army is a bit too overpriced, and the building itself is usually kind of grimy. Not only that, but I'm part of the Clubsavers, where I get an email when there is 50% off the whole store. This sale happens twice a year, and it really helps me save money! The other thing I use a lot would be Kijiji. I am someone who not only buys from Kijiji, but I am also a seller. I have sold things I do not need, like my flute and ukulele. This way, you can make money off things that you don't use, and you declutter your room. Something that I would advise, if you are selling or buying things on Kijiji, would be to meet up at a public place. I do not feel comfortable just texting a bunch of people my address and cell number, especially when some of them never reply.

If you are buying a cell phone, make sure to research what a real one is supposed to look like. I have bought 2 iPhones on Kijiji. I always make sure to meet at the Apple store or somewhere with Wi-Fi, because you can check the serial number of the phone to see if it is blacklisted. Blacklisted is when someone's phone is stolen, and they report it to the carrier, who then does something so your stolen phone cannot use SIM cards. Kijiji has a built-in chat room, which is a lot nicer than having to email each other or give out your cell number. Whenever I sell items, I always put in a fake address, and write *please contact* for location. Make sure to stay firm with your pricing, because there are people who will try and low-ball you. At the same time, don't assign a ridiculously high price, because no one will contact you. Even though it takes me more time to find cheaper items by using Kijiji, I think it is worth it if it saves you money!

Notes

Notes

Chapter 3

Save

Start At a Young Age

You could start saving up money from a young age. I think it's important for parents to teach their children how to use their money when they are given money. If you're given an allowance as a child, you could put half of it away and spend the other half. If you started to get an allowance from age ten, and you have saved until you're 18—let's say you're given $20 a month, which becomes $240 per year, and you save half of that—it's $140! If you do that for 8 years, it's $1100! This may not seem like a lot of money, but it's a great place to start at. The hardest thing to do is to start saving, but once you start, it becomes easier to do.

Another way to save up money when you're little is to not spend money your parents give to you for holidays. This way, you can buy a big ticket item instead of something that you might play with for a few minutes. I think it's important for parents to teach their kids good learning habits, and once they start to save up money, they have a bigger chance of being successful. Even if your parents have taught you how to save money at a young age, you can start to save up yourself!! If you have any siblings, you could be the one to let them become aware of their money! As already mentioned, some people are not financially literate and have no idea how to spend their money. But this is not their fault, as they were never taught by their parents how to be smart with their money.

You are never too old to learn something new. My mom started learning about how to save money in her late 30s, which shows how you can start saving money at any age. I congratulate you for taking the initiative to read this book and become SMART with your money. Think back to your own childhood. Did you parents buy you anything you wanted, or did you have to earn toys? My mom was more focused on the reward you get for good behaviour. On YouTube, you can see that there are a lot of videos of children acting out because their parents did not buy them what they wanted. Do you remember how you were as a child? Some parents are incapable of telling their children no, and this results in spoiled children. If you ever have children, then you can teach them to save money from a young age!

Limit Your Spending

As a teen, it can seem difficult to limit how much you are spending. Something that I find that can make it easier is creating goals or rules that you have to follow. You could create a rule that you can only go out once a week. This means either going out with friends or family, when you go to a restaurant. It could also mean just buying fast food or buying one item, either at a mall or online. If you limit yourself to spending your money on every Friday after school, it will make you look forward to the end of the week.

Save

At the same time, this shouldn't be an excuse to spend all your money on Friday. I mean, limit it to spending a certain amount of money, like $30, so you have enough for one meal, and $20 to spend on a shirt or something. I personally switch between going out once a week and limiting myself to a certain amount of money per week. Each person is different, and you're going to have to find which technique works for you. I'm not the only person in my family who does the once-a-week technique. My mom does it as well—every weekend, I go out with my family to a restaurant that costs around $10–$15 per person. Ever since I turned 18, I now pay for myself at restaurants, and so does the rest of my family. This might not be the case for you, as you might not have a job, or your parents may just have a different parenting style.

I find that I spend the most money when I feel lazy. Let's say I'm at my college campus, and I have been studying for a while, and I'm hungry. I usually end up eating in the overpriced cafeteria. I have noticed that due to the convenience of the cafeteria, I have been buying my food for 5 days at school, instead of taking the time to make myself a lunch. Everyone does make mistakes, and I don't expect you to immediately start using my methods without hiccups. I, myself, have spent money on things I could've made at home or didn't need. If you are someone who spends a lot of money, it might be easier to start with a smaller goal. Instead of spending money every single day, you could spend money every other day. As mentioned, do whatever helps you become successful at saving money. Recently, I have returned to buying food at the grocery store and prepping meals the night before. This saves me up to $12 a day!

Buy Generic Brands

Another way to save money is by buying generic brands. Believe it or not, some factories produce generic and brand names in the same factory! Something you can do to see if there is a difference between the name brand and generic is to look at the nutrition facts. You can compare not only the ingredients but also how much sugar, calories, and fat there is. For some necessities, like salt, toilet paper, or sugar, it's better to pick the generic brand, because these products contain few ingredients.

Another thing that can save you a lot of money is to buy generic brand medicines. These generic brands go through a lot of regulatory testing to make sure they are not only safe for use but also effective. Ibuprofen is a good example of something that a lot of people use. Another drug for which I would recommend getting the generic brand would be allergy medication. I personally have allergies, and the medication can be very expensive! My mom likes to buy cooking supplies, like baking soda, broth, and pancake mix. These are really basic items that can help in recipes. Something that I personally avoid would be the more important items, like pet food, or any human food that isn't basic, like sugar. An example of this would be that I never buy generic chocolate, because you can get name brand chocolate for 60 cents at the dollar store.

Not only that, but you can definitely taste the difference in the quality of the chocolate. I would never buy generic pet food because I see my cat as my own child. Even though it's cheap, think about the fillers they use in the cat food to keep the price low. My vet has warned me to never get cheap pet food because it can cause problems like obesity and urinary tract infections.

Save

You should also not buy generic brand coffee. I know a lot of teens drink coffee, and the quality of generic brand coffee would make it taste like dirt. Finally, the last thing that I suggest you do not buy with a generic brand, would be technology. This is because you get what you pay for. If you buy a cheap laptop, then you're going to have a laptop that has a slow processor, a bad resolution for the screen, and no customer service if the machine breaks down. In summary, generic brands should be bought for items that are basic and have few ingredients, but you should never buy generic brands for things that can have many fillers in them to keep the price cheap.

Separate Your Money

So, I have gone on and on about how to save money, but where do you put that money that you're saving up? The first thing you can do is use separation. This means that you have a different bank account for the money that you spend and save. It's really easy to set up. I personally use TD bank, and there they will happily set up another bank account. If you are under 18 years old, then you can have a youth account. This type of account has no fees, and you would not be allowed to have a credit card without a guardian's permission.

Once you turn 18, which is the legal age in Canada, you have to change your account. If you decide to go to post-secondary school, you can get a student account, which also has no fees. Once you set up the two accounts, you'll have one that is called chequing, and one that is called savings. The savings account can have an interest rate, so you build interest on the amount you're saving up. With a chequing account, you can give cheques from that account. A cheque is a piece of paper that you would give to the bank, and they would add the amount that is on the cheque. Something that can feel really daunting is getting a credit card when you turn 18. I think it's important to get a credit card because you will need it to build your credit score. A credit score is what the bank rates you out of 900 when you pay your bills on time. So if you were to be late on a payment, then your score goes down.

It's important to build a credit score because when you are older and you want to rent a house or take out a mortgage, they will check your credit score to see if you're responsible enough to pay them back. You would also need your credit score for when you buy or rent a car. To get back to the topic of separating your money, if you can't see the amount that you're saving, you won't spend it! Another way that you can separate your money is to put the amount that you are allowed to spend, in the account. So if you have a goal of $50, then you put $50 in your account. This may be embarrassing if you go to buy something and your card is declined, but it should remind you that you are over your budget for that week, and it can also serve to teach you what happens when you go over the limit.

Make Saving Money a Habit

How can you be successful in saving your money? Make it a habit! Maybe you could start with putting $10 in a jar. This is easier to do because you can see the actual amount of money accumulate over time, versus putting it into a bank account. If it's easier, you can put a certain amount of money every month. This way, you know that each month you need to have a certain amount of money available to put in your savings account.

Save

This can also help prepare you for when you're an adult. This is because, when you're an adult, you need to have a certain amount of money saved to pay bills. Once you get older, a lot of the money you make will have to go to paying for your housing, food, clothes, and necessities. Even as a teenager, I have some bills. I have a bill for Crunchyroll (Anime), a YouTube premium (video and music), and my phone bill. This would be my monthly bills, and then I have Amazon Prime, which is a yearly bill. I also have to pay for my cat's vet bills, food, and toys. If you have bills, make sure to keep track of them! Another thing you should do is reward good habits. If you are able to keep putting away money each month until it becomes a habit, you should reward yourself by treating yourself; you could get your nails done, buy a new pair of shoes, or even have a facial.

You can also apply this technique to everyday activities. Another way to make saving a habit is to set reminders in your phone. Another thing you should be aware of is that a habit doesn't just happen straight away. You might have some setbacks, where you either don't have the money to put in the account or you forget to put it in on the right day. You can either just put it in the next day, put double the amount the next day it's due, or let it slide and accept that everyone makes mistakes. It's important to create reminders on your phone. You can be reminded in case you forgot to put in the amount of money you wanted to save. If you wanted to work out, you would set a time that you have to do it, create a chart, and put a checkmark every time you did it. This will be touched more upon in the *Track* section.

Save Money With a Friend

How can you make it easier on yourself to save money? The final thing you can do is save money with a friend. This way, you could compete with one another. Not only could you cheer each other on, but you both understand what you're going through, especially when you make a mistake. So if you have a goal of spending $50 a week, and so does your friend, and if you guys go out together, you can remind each other that you don't need that new pair of shoes or a cute phone case.

I personally make sure to tell my friends when I go out that I have a certain amount of money I want to spend. Sometimes when I'm shopping, I ask my friends if I should buy something, and because they know I want to spend a certain amount, they would say that I shouldn't buy it. Not only that, but friends are a good support system when you feel like you're not being very successful. Some people would talk to their parents about their financial goals. I bet yours would be supportive of your decisions, because it would help you in the future! If I go shopping with my mom, she'll usually say that it is something I don't need, and it will take up room in the house, but sometimes it's actually a good investment. An example of this would be when I got a new backpack because my old one was ripped. This would be something that I would use every day for school, and my friend would totally agree that it's worth the money—especially because I got a backpack, which usually costs $120–$200, for $40, thanks to Amazon.

Another investment that I found useful would be paying for an Amazon Prime membership. Fun fact: if you are a student, you can get Amazon Prime for half the price—$40 per year. This is

Save

definitely worth the amount, as I buy a lot of items on Amazon, and the one to two day free shipping saves me a lot of money since it would usually be around $7 per item. When you are competing with friends, you are helping each other by supporting one another. It's always good to have a support system when you're trying to better your life. In this case, it would be saving up money. If you and your friend are able to hit goals, like saving $500, you could go and do something together: maybe skating, watching a movie, or even going to an amusement park.
.

Notes

Save

Notes

Notes

Chapter 4

Make Money

Do Errands For Family and Friends

The next letter in the acronym is **M**, which stands for *make money*. For those of you who are younger and are unable to obtain a job, there are others ways to make money. The first thing you can do to make income is to do things for your family. Perhaps you could get $5 every time you clean your room, vacuum the carpets, or cut the grass. Another way you can get income from your parents would be through an allowance. Not all parents provide their children with an allowance. If your parents don't give you an allowance, then you can try and convince them to give you one, or just do chores around the house to get money. I think it's important to maintain a good relationship with your parents.

If your parents don't give you an allowance, or don't want to pay you, then you should try and convince them to. Because you have the intention to save the money, you could say that you want to earn money so you can learn how to deal with money. This would include how to responsibly use that money or save it. Let's say your parents are totally against paying you any money; the next way to make money is to get it from an outside source. This could be raking the leaves for a neighbour, baby sitting, or even dog walking. Babysitting is a hit or miss; either you will find someone who is trustworthy, has well behaved kids, and is laid back, or you might have a stressful day, where you have to deal with a badly behaved kid. I think, for your first job, you should try and babysit someone's child that you know.

This could be one of your parent's friends, your friend's sibling, or even your own sibling. It can be a bit scary babysitting a child in an unknown house. This is why I suggest using your house if your own parents are okay with it. The nice thing about dog walking is that you could do it only locally, so you'd be walking the dog in your own neighbourhood. This seems like less of a task if you like dogs. Just make sure not to have too many leashes.

Get a Part-Time Job, Learn Independence and New Skills

You're now old enough to get a part time job, or your parents finally gave you permission to start working. The hardest part of working is finding the job. When you apply to a job, you need to present a cover letter and resume. In the cover letter, you would list basic info, like your name, address, phone number, accomplishments, and characteristics. The resume elaborates on your strengths, weaknesses, and why you are a perfect match for this job. Some managers will not even read the resume, while some will look at every detail of the resume. Everyone has had a different experience of getting hired. For me, I applied to 3–4 places that either never got back to me or said they weren't hiring. The last place I visited had a hiring sign, so I went in and asked to speak to the manager. He asked when I was available, to which I replied, "Any day," and he then told me to show up tomorrow to start staff training.

Some people will have a really easy time getting a job, because of their connections. Maybe your sister has a job at Macdonald's, and when there's an opening, you are given the position. Something that I'm grateful for, thanks to my job, is the skills that I have learned. This would include how to respond to angry customers, how to work under pressure, and how to collaborate with others. In some jobs, you may learn skills like how to use a cash register, how to count money, and how to communicate with guests. Another positive of having a job is the independence that you gain from a job. You work, get money, put money in a bank account, or spend it. You also are responsible for your actions. This means that if a customer is yelling at you, you self-regulate, stay professional, and let them get their anger out before speaking. If you are late to your shift, or don't keep track of the schedule and miss an entire shift, your manager will not be happy with you, and this may even result in you getting fired.

Some jobs even have perks, like 50% off the product you sell, or even free damaged products. In summary, I think a part time job is an important milestone that has a lot of benefits, like making an income, learning new skills, and gaining independence. The only consequence I see is the amount of effort and time you put into work. Just know that the more effort you put in, the more you will be rewarded.

Sell Your Skills

If you don't want to work for someone else, then you can work for yourself. If you're good at doing something, then take advantage of it and make your own business. An example of this would be if you're good at knitting; then you could make an account on Etsy, take pictures of the items you can make, and start to sell the items. You could also sell a service. If you're good at painting, maybe you could do face painting at birthday parties. You could even do a bake sale or lemonade stand, if you're good at cooking.

The nice thing about selling your skills or services is that you're your own boss. This means you don't have to follow someone else's orders, and you get to decide how much and how long you work. But at the same time, it can be challenging to regulate yourself so you are productive and not wasting time on YouTube. An example I can give is similar to when you have to decide when to work on school work, versus hanging out with friends and family. When you own your own business, things can become challenging, as you also have to keep track of the expenses. Getting back to the knitting example, if you have a customer who wants a hand knit scarf, you have to determine a price based on how much the materials were, and the amount of labour it took to create the item.

You would also have to deal with the people who want you to make things for free. This kind of person usually thinks that they're doing you a favour by bringing attention to your business. I personally would either ignore this type of person or list my price for my services and not reply. Etsy is a good website to use because you don't have to pay for your own website, create one, or even try and find customers. Clients seek you out because they know they can find handmade items on Etsy. I personally have bought many things from Etsy, like handmade earrings and a matching necklace.

Sell Things You Don't Want!
(Get money and more space)

The next way that you can make money is by selling things you don't want. Every season, I make sure to go through my closet and put the clothes I do not use in a garbage bag. I then bring this bag to a second hand store, like Value Village. The nice thing about donating clothes is that you not only free up space in your house but you also are doing something eco-friendly. Instead of throwing out clothes that are never worn—which is a waste—you are letting them be re-used. Not only that, but these thrift stores usually give you a coupon or a store credit. It's not just clothes that you can donate; you can donate anything that is in decent shape: tables, coats, toys, and more.

Thrift stores are also good because you can buy items for half the price. This is not only good for those who are trying to save money, but also for those who are less fortunate. Something that is even more amazing would be the variety of clothing styles that are available at thrift stores. There is even clothing from different areas of the world. Another way that can make you more money would be by using websites like Kijiji or Craigslist to resell things. I used Kijiji when I wanted to sell big ticket items like a flute, backpack, or even my old laptop. I usually am able to get a decent price.

I would try aiming for half of the current retail price. The Kijiji app does make it easier to communicate with one another. I would advise not giving out personal information like where you live, and also keep the name to your first name. Always make sure to meet up in a public place. This is not only for your own safety but also for the safety of the buyer. When you are about to buy the product, make sure to inspect it thoroughly for any scratches. If it's a phone, ask if it comes with any accessories, like phone cases, and make sure that it turns on and is the authentic brand. If you're looking at a specific brand, there are videos on YouTube to show you how to identify a counterfeit product.

Have a Website Pay You!

There are apps, like Carrot, which reward you with points for playing games, doing surveys, and just spending money. If you want to collect Scene points, Carrot lets you set up walking goals, and if you are able to maintain the goal, then you are awarded with points. Another way to earn money online would be with Swagbucks. Swagbucks gives users points for answering surveys. After you collect a certain amount of points, you are able to redeem a gift card. I personally have used Carrots, and it's a good way to earn Scene points just for walking until you hit your daily goal.

Some people may want to cheat the system by setting super low goals so they are always able to reach their goals. I think doing this ruins the whole idea of hard work paying off. I find that doing general surveys, like what you think of a certain company, or demographic surveys, are safe and easy to answer. I would not recommend you filling out any survey where they ask personal info, like where you live or your credit card number. This could become a fraud case. The final way that you could earn money or rewards would be by writing reviews. I'm someone that buys a lot of things online, and I notice that a lot of companies contact me if I don't write a review.

This usually takes me a minute to do, and I'm happy to do so. This is because it not only helps the company if you gave a good review, but you're also helping people who want to know how good the restaurant is. I know for a fact that I always check reviews for an item before buying it, to make sure that it is worth the money and that the quality of the item is good.

Reward Programs, Scene Points, PC Optimum points, Loyalty Programs, Air Miles

The last way that you can earn money is by using rewards programs. Rewards programs are programs that reward customers for their loyalty to the brand. Examples of this would include a Scene movie card, PC Optimum Points, and Air Miles. For Scene points, if you scan at the supporting retail places, every $1 you spend is equivalent to 3 points. But at the movie theatre, if you buy one general admission ticket, you would get 100 points.

With the Scene card, you can redeem your points: for every 1000 points you have, you can either redeem a free movie or $10. The nice thing about using reward programs is that it doesn't take long to register, you are doing nothing extra to use this card, and you can redeem points to get free products or money. Some people may be worried about all the cards you would have to carry if you registered for every single rewards program, but a lot of cards have gone digital now. On the iPhone, there is an app that has the barcode of cards like the Scene card, which the cash register would scan when you go to that certain store.

This also means that your wallet is lighter, and you'll never forget your cards again. I notice that a lot of clients forget their Scene card, or they spend time trying to find their physical card, or are trying to open the app with no Wi-Fi. A loyalty program that I would recommend for adults would be the PC Optimum Points. This is because you can get points from Loblaws, No Frills, and Shoppers Drug Mart. These are all stores that I go to, and my mom gets around $100 in free grocery store money. It's something that doesn't take a lot of effort to do. You don't have to go out of your way to answer a survey or make your own business; it's a passive way to make money.

There are also reward programs where you buy a coffee 4 times and then get a small drink of your choice. This is also applicable to the very successful Starbucks reward card. For this program, you can only earn stars by using an app. If you reach 150 stars, then you become a gold star member. This incentive of becoming part of an *elite* group means that more people are more likely to spend their money to reach that goal. In summary, reward programs are a good passive way to earn money by redeeming points; but keep track of how many you have, by using an app online.

Make Money

Notes

Notes

Chapter 5

Analyze

Think Before You Buy

Now that you know how to save and make money, I'm going to teach you how to spend it wisely. To begin with, the first thing you have to do before buying is to pause before buying something. Let's give an example of something that you don't really need, but you want it. Let's say it's a really cute purse that costs $70; it's from a department store, so it's $70 instead of $120. It's also from the name brand, Guess. Do you buy it? Before buying, think about how long it will take you to pay it back. For me, I have a job where I'm payed $14/hour. So $70 is equal to 5 hours of labour, which is one day of work. For me, personally, it's worth buying it. This is because I use a purse every time I go out; and not only that, but it's bigger than the one I have currently, which will benefit me—the older I get, the bigger the purse I seem to need.

So that means I would be using this product every time I go out. Not only that, but I'd save $50 because I'm at a department store. After looking at all these factors, I could conclude that I should buy this. If it was the original price of $120, I might want to sleep on it. Sleeping on it is when you give yourself the time to reflect whether you really need the item you're looking at. If you still think about it the next day, and it's worth the time it takes to travel back to the mall, then get it. The only risk, when you sleep on it, is that you risk it getting sold. Let's do an example of it being an online item.

One of the pros of buying online is that you don't have to travel anywhere; and not only that, but the website will warn you if it's low in stock. Let's say you see a pair of sneakers online, and they're Louis Vuitton, so they cost around $750. You think they look pretty cool, but you hesitate because of the price. Before you even consider buying that item, ask yourself a few questions: 1. Do you have a source of income available to make that amount of money? 2. Will you be using these every day? 3. What could you buy instead of the item? If you say, "Yes, I have a job, but I'm paid minimum wage, and I would not be wearing this pair of shoes because they will be part of my shoe collection, where they will spend their time in a clear box.

Just from that alone, I can conclude for you that this is not a smart purchase. Instead of spending that $750 on shoes, you could buy a phone, a plane ticket, a laptop, a gaming system plus games, or 6 pairs of shoes that cost $120 each. Look at all the things you could buy instead; you could even buy the Nintendo Switch, which costs $375, plus 4 games, which cost $80 each. These are the actual prices of these products from Amazon.ca. Now that you've taken that second to think before buying, it's time to figure out if you really need it.

Analyze

Do You Really Need It?
(Will you not be able to function without it?)

Most items that teens buy are not things that you need to survive. At our age, the things we buy are usually for pleasure. I know this because I recently bought myself a Nintendo 2DS with 3 games. This was around $395. I figured out how often I would be playing this console, which would save me data as I use it when I don't have Wi-Fi on trips. Not only that, but for each game, I spend around 20–40 hours, and this is because I've been playing Pokémon games. The Nintendo 2DS is only $100 cheaper. If I had analyzed this closer, I would have realized that it would be smarter to buy the newer Nintendo gaming system, as it would have a bigger screen and could be played on the TV. Because I took the time to analyze that I could afford to buy this item, I had to figure out if I needed it.

Obviously, a gaming system is not something I need to survive, and it is purely there for entertainment. So I conclude that I do not need this item; I want it. The next thing I have to analyze is if I deserve it. So, I got this device after completing my first college semester—my lowest mark being a 74—and from that, I decided I should reward myself for my hard work, and I bought it. This may seem kind of egotistical, trying to figure out if you did something good to deserve to buy something. It can be especially challenging if you are judging yourself. Maybe you could make a chart of what you have done so far to deserve a gaming console. This could be from academic accomplishments to personal goals, like working out every other day for a month. If you really need help judging if you deserve a wanted item, try asking your parents or friends if they think you should buy it.

Maybe they have a different view point. For your parents, maybe you haven't kept your room clean. If this is the case, clean your room, and then buy the gaming console. An example of something that you need to buy would be something like toilet paper and toothpaste, and for women, menstrual products. Usually your parents will cover these basic needs, but sometimes they won't. Because I'm in college, but I'm living at home, my mom has decided to pay for my food and the house amenities. This means I have to buy pads, toothpaste, dental floss, and essentials for my cat. I own my cat and take responsibly for him. This means I feed him, brush him, and clean his litter. Not only that, but I pay for his food, brushes, and vet bills. These are all examples of things that my cat needs to survive—the things he wants would be items like treats and toys. Not only that, but I do buy him a sweater or collars.

How Long Will It Take To Get the Money Back That You're Going to Spend, and How?

As you have noticed, I have used basic math to help me figure out how long it will take to pay back an amount. I'm going to break down an example of how long it will take to pay it back. This is an especially important skill for buying big ticket items. Let's say you are looking to buy the Samsung Galaxy S9, which in Canada costs around $720. Now, if you have a job that pays you minimum wage, which is $14, and you work 15 hours a week, you can calculate how much money you make each week. $14x15=$210. If $210 is what you are paid per week, you then divide 720 by 210, which is 3.4 weeks. So, you'd pay off buying this phone in 4 weeks. We then can look at how long you'd be using this phone.

Analyze

Most phone plans are two years, so I'm going to put the lifespan of this phone at 2 years. It can usually be more, depending on whether you lose or break the phone. So, comparing 1 month's pay, versus at least 24 months of use, it is clear that this phone is definitely worth buying. I don't think you need to do these calculations on items under $40. You can do the basic math that one hour of labour is $14, and not have to divide anything. I think figuring out how long it will take to pay something back is important to do because it helps you realize how much effort you have to put in to buy something. This can also stop you from buying on impulse because you realize that money does not grow on trees, and this technique can stop you from splurging. I personally take the time to write this all down, because having a visual to look at can help you make the decision.

The longer something takes to pay back, then the more you should look at if you really need it. Once you get older and you start to look at big ticket items, like housing and a car, they split up the billing into monthly payments, where you don't have to pay it outright. I think you should always choose the shortest plan to pay back for a car. This is because you should be able to pay for at least 50% of the initial price of the car. Otherwise, it's pretty obvious you can't afford that car, and not only that, but as soon as you drive that car out of the lot, the car decreases in value. Car companies also release a model of the car every single year, so you should make sure that you don't get stuck in a 10-year contract for a car.

Is It Worth It?

The next thing you should do before buying something is to figure out if it's worth the effort that you put in to create that amount of money. The easiest way you can do this is by asking questions, like how long you will use it. How often will you use it, and finally, is it a one- time use item? Let's use the example where you want to buy a new laptop. You have decided on the model and brand that you want to buy. Let's say it's the MacBook laptop. The laptop that you have right now only plays sound when you use headphones. It also is really slow. Thanks to this, you have already decided that you have to buy a new laptop. You already know that you can afford $1,500, because it will take you 7 and a half weeks to pay it off. Now it's time to think about whether it's worth the giant price tag. How often will you use this laptop?

Personally, for me, I would be using this laptop every single day. I use it for education, work, and entertainment. For school, I use my laptop to type my notes, and also to organize my to-do list or schedule. There are also a lot of programs that I use for school, like Microsoft Word, Excel, and PowerPoint. I can also search how to do things on the web, open and print class lessons, and even work on a group project with classmates. I sometimes use my laptop for work when I need to communicate with colleagues. As for entertainment, I use my laptop to watch Anime, TV shows, and a lot of YouTube. I also have a few games on my laptop, like GTA 5 and the Sims 4.

This item has multiple uses and is essential for me personally to succeed academically. Another thing you can figure out in regard to the worth of the item is how long it will last. The average lifespan of a laptop is around 3 to 5 years. If it takes 2 months to pay it off, and you're using it for around 36–60 months, it's definitely worth the price. The last thing you have to do to see if it's worth buying the laptop, would be to look at the quality of the product. The Apple company is a well-known brand that is known for having high quality material. With clothing, you can feel the quality of the clothes. I think that it's worth paying more money for a higher quality item because it not only works better, but it also lasts longer, which increases the value of the product.

Are You Able To Afford It?

The final thing you should make sure of is if you can afford it, even if you have figured out how long it takes to make up the amount of money, and that the item you have bought has value. As the previous page explained, it would take you two months to pay back the amount. Because you're a teenager, you don't have a lot of expenses. When you're calculating how long it would take to pay back the amount, you are not taking any bills or fees into account. For example, because I'm an older teen, I have a few bills that I must pay each month. This includes $7 for Crunchyroll, and $75 for my phone bill. As you get older, you will have even more things you have to pay for, such as rent, food, Wi-Fi, or cable and other necessities.

Once you go into college or university, and live on your own, you have to weigh if you want to eat or play a game. I think it's important to have to pay for your own expenses because you learn how to be independent. If you don't have any bills to pay, think about all the other things you buy each month. You can make a chart and figure out just how much money you are spending. For example, if you spend $20 a week just on junk food, $50 on essentials like toothpaste or pads, and another $30 on entertainment, you need to count this in regard to how much money you need to save. This way, by including everything that you spend your money on can show you if you really can afford something. As you have already figured out how to calculate how much time it will take to pay off the amount an item costs, you should make sure to always question if you can afford it, especially if it's a higher priced item. I would consider anything over $100 as a high priced item.

This is because $100 is equivalent to a full time work day of 7 1/2 hours. I personally work around 4 to 5 hours per shift, so for teens it would take 2 days to pay off $100, not one. The final way to figure out if you can afford to buy something is to make sure, if you had to pay off the amount it costs all at once, you can do so. I have talked about how long it would take to pay it off, but you should have $1500 in your bank account to pay off the debt immediately. This can be different when it comes to buying a house, but you should still have enough to pay 50–60% of the full price. If you're 18, and you own a credit card, make sure that whatever you buy on your credit card, you can pay it back immediately with your normal bank account. Something that I do is to use the TD app to pay the bill immediately after buying the item. I use my credit card because I have cash back of 1%. I think it's really important to know how much money you have, so you know how much you can spend.

Analyze

Notes

Notes

Chapter 6

Research

Read Reviews to Check the Quality

You know how to save, spend, and make money, but how do you decide where to buy something? To begin with, when buying an item, you should be looking at the reviews. If you're inside a store, you can search on your phone to see what other people think of it. If you are buying an item online, then it's a lot easier to look at reviews. On Amazon, it displays the ranking of the product. I personally don't buy anything unless it has at least 4 out of 5 stars. When it comes to big ticket items, I usually tend to buy things with a rating of 4.5–5 stars. When you're reading the reviews, you have to look at a one star review so you can see what possible issues can occur with the product.

Sometimes the person who reviewed the item is giving it a bad ranking because it either never showed up or it shipped late. Another big issue that can happen is that it is breaking in the first week. If you see any review about it breaking easily or not lasting long, then you should look at another product. The website that you are on sometimes doesn't even have any reviews, so you might have to look at a different website. There are also those who give it a rating without commenting. If someone leaves a comment, it either means that something was so good or so horrible that the person went out of their way to review it. An example of something that I almost bought but didn't, because of the reviews, would be when I was looking at Bluetooth earbuds. At the time, I had broken my current pair, so I now had to look through the hundreds of results on Amazon.

One of the contenders that I considered buying had multiple reviews, where one of the earbuds had stopped working, and not only that, but communication with the seller was really bad. Because of the possibility of malfunctioning earbuds, with no customer service, I decided I should not risk buying them. Something you should be wary of is commercials. This is because the people who review the product are either paid actors or the company has only put together the positive reviews.

This is usually seen on *As Seen on TV* commercials, where someone says how great the product is and how they can't live without it. Another way to find if a product is worth buying is by getting info from friends and family. I am more likely to buy something if my mom praises how good the product is. Word of mouth is something that is really important for businesses, including restaurants. If all the reviews on google maps for a restaurant or business is 4.5 stars, then people are more likely to visit.

Price Check Using Websites

Let's say you're thinking of buying something at Walmart, but you want to make sure you're getting the best deal. Adults may look through flyers to *price check* the item. But for us teens, it can be even faster by using websites like Price Grabber. This website allows you to either type in a specific product or browse their categories for an item. A website that is even better than Price Grabber would be ShopBot. This website doesn't just compare prices for you, but it also shows the ranking from reviews, and the pros and cons of the item. I think this website is also a lot more user friendly. The final website that is really important is Google Shopping. This has more variety then the other sites because it uses Google's huge search engine. Sometimes items either go on sale or it's listed on their website.

I had this happen to me when I went to Giant Tiger to get stocking stuffers. I got Terry's chocolate orange for $5, only to go to Walmart to find them for $4. This annoyed me more than really affecting my spending. One dollar isn't enough to be upset over, and I certainly wasn't going to go all the way back to Giant Tiger. But this serves as an example that no matter how much you try to save money, there will sometimes be surprises that you can't predict. An example of when I saved a lot of money, thanks to researching, would be when I was looking for a new backpack for college. I was interested in the brand, Doughnut, because it's a better version of fjallraven Kanken. This is because it has shoulder straps and an organizer included. How did I find this out? I watched people compare the two bags, and I read online reviews. After figuring out that Doughnut was the brand I wanted to go with, I then looked at the models. I eventually picked out the Macaroon style and started to search on Amazon for pricing. Doughnut is a brand from Hong Kong, making it even more expensive and difficult to find.

I found the price to be around $120–$200. This is obviously a lot of money, and I decided to not buy it as it wasn't worth the price tag. I then searched *laptop college backpack*. I then saw one for

$40 that looked exactly like the Doughnut backpack. I bought it and, when I received it, it turned out that it was an official Doughnut backpack! This is an example of how you should try researching something with different terminology. You might just find it under another name! As already mentioned, some places have price matching, where they will match a competitor's price. If you find someone who has a better price, you fill out a form on their website and include a copy of the competitor's pricing. This can be taking a picture of an ad or screenshotting a website.

Research On the Go With Apps like ScanLife, ShopSavvy, etc., That Scan the Barcode

If you go shopping, and you want to use my method of researching when in a mall, what happens if the product you want doesn't have a sign saying the name, so you can't compare prices because you can't research the product. Well, I have a way to compare prices, as long as there is a barcode. There should always be a barcode; otherwise, how else would you pay for it? You can use an app called BuyVia. This app lets you scan codes to get info about both the product and prices! I, myself, have used it, and it takes only a few seconds for the item to scan. Once it scans the item, it tells you the name of the product and where you can buy it.

From there, you can use the name of the product to search even more to find info on reviews and prices. This app is available on both iPhones and Android. You login to Facebook so it can remember the things you search. I use this app for almost everything. An example of how to use it would be that you first scan the item, and it will take you to the name of the product and

Research

where to buy it. It also lists the ratings and reviews. On this app, you can also search stores for deals. This app lets you research prices even faster than looking through catalogues or looking online. This is also applicable to hotels or flights. There are websites like Trivago and Kayak, where you search once and it compares everything for you.

This might not be something that concerns you as a teenager, but it's nice to know about it so you can tell your parents when you're going on a family vacation, or when you want to travel with friends. I personally, as a teen, use Kayak and Trivago when I'm trying to plan an outing with my family for the summer. This way, I can compare all the prices and save money by looking at the cheapest days to fly. Another way to save money abroad is to use websites like Airbnb. This is when you live in someone's house. This is usually cheaper than staying at a hotel because it's owned by local people. Not only that, but you feel more like a local then a tourist. When my family went to Paris, we stayed in an Airbnb for a few nights, which was a lot cheaper than a hotel, and we were close to a bakery.

Find Coupons/Promo Codes Online

The next way you can save money is by using coupons. Don't worry; you're not going to have to be like one of those people on TLC's Extreme Couponing (unless you want to), where you only buy things with coupons. The problem with this is that the people are only buying things that they usually don't need. An example of this would be when a man had a stock pile of menstrual items, even though there were no women in the house. He bought them because they were cheap. I'm not telling you to save up a ridiculous amount of coupons that have nothing to do with what you want to purchase. Instead, I'm going to teach you to use coupons for the things you really want to buy.

Let's say you're on SoftMoc, and you want to buy a nice pair of shoes. Before you press *Confirm Order*, you should google *SoftMoc coupons 2018*. A website called RetailMeNot will pop up, and it will provide a bunch of promo codes that you will have to manually put in and see if it works. I ended up finding one that saved me 20% off my order, and this only took me 5 minutes to save $20, which I think is well worth it. You can also get discounts if you provide your email to get a newsletter. When you do get the email, you just scroll to the bottom and click on unsubscribe. This way you can easily get out of the daily emails, while saving money. A faster way to find promo codes would be by using Honey.

Honey is a browser extension for google chrome. When you're on a certain website, like Walmart, you would click on *Find Coupons*, and it will give you a list of coupons that you can try out to see if they work. This way you don't have to look on multiple coupon websites, because Honey looks at the websites for you. The final website that has both promo codes and huge discounts would be Groupon. I have used this website many times for services like massages, manicures, and even laser hair removal. You can also use this website for entertainment, like laser tag, amusement park tickets, and subscription boxes. Whatever you can think of, Groupon will usually have a deal for you. Let's say you want to buy a Groupon for a manicure. You'd pay for the Groupon, and then you would call the store (number is given), make an appointment, and redeem the voucher. You redeem the voucher by screenshotting a picture of a barcode after agreeing that you can't return the voucher once you've seen it. This way of researching takes a lot less effort because you don't have to search around for a promo code.

See If You Can Buy It Used for a Lower Price

Another thing you should research before buying an item would be to see if you can buy it used. This is part of the Save model, where you could use the website Kijiji or Craigslist to see if anyone has the item for a better price. I have researched if there were used iPhones on Kijiji. When I was in grade 11, the phone I had was stolen. Because of this, I had to buy a new one, and I didn't want to spend $600–$1000 on a new phone, so I looked on Kijiji for people who didn't want their own. I ended up buying one for $300, which had 64GB and was in decent condition. As already mentioned, you should always do the deal in a public place. So I met the person in front of the Apple store. Once they arrived, they took out the phone, and I then inspected it. I know enough about Apple counterfeits to know that a real iPhone has a star screw beside the speaker. If you do not know much about an actual iPhone, then you need to do some research to make sure you don't get duped.

You can watch YouTube videos to learn what a real iPhone's packaging looks like. Another thing you can do is to put in the serial number (found under settings) on Apple's website, which will tell you that it's either blacklisted, fake, or an official Apple iPhone. Thanks to putting in the time to save money, I actually did. I know that doing research can seem kind of taxing, especially if you only save a little amount. If you don't want to take the time to research, that is your own decision, and I respect that. Just don't be surprised when your friend gets it cheaper, or you learn that the phone you got on Kijiji was a fake. I think it's important to at least know what the official product looks like. There are a lot of videos online that can help educate you on the fake items. This knowledge can be applied to a lot of expensive name brands, like Apple, Gucci, Jordan, Nike, and Samsung. You should also make sure to pay attention to the condition of the used items.

Something that I personally avoid buying is refurbished items, unless it's from the official seller. So, if you see a refurbished dell laptop on the dell website, go ahead and buy it. But if you see a $1000 laptop for $400 on some random website, I would not trust buying it. A big problem with buying used or even new items online is the chance of being ripped off. They might send you a rock in the Apple iPhone case, or even junk. This is why I don't use eBay, as it can be pretty sketchy. The same goes for websites like aliExpress and Wish. I don't recommend buying technology on their websites. This is why it's smarter to use websites like Kijiji, where you see the product in person, and they can't rip you off.

In Store vs Online, Pros and Cons

The last thing that I want to touch upon is buying things in store versus online. The positives of buying things in store include being able to actually touch the item to feel the quality, try it on if its clothes, or have an idea of how much room it will take up. Also, if you buy the item in a store, you are immediately given it. Things that I buy in store would include food, clothing, and technology. I find trying to buy clothing online is challenging because you have to use a tape measure and try to accurately measure your dimensions and see what size you are, and not only

Research

that, but a lot of stores have different sizing. I might be an XS in one store but a S in another. Because I have emphasized how important it is to compare prices or find a better price online, I would first see the item in real life. So, when I was going to buy the Dell XPS 13, I went to a Microsoft store to check out the actual device. It's a lot easier seeing the quality of the screen or feeling how heavy the laptop is than reading the dimensions and weight info. Another great thing about buying in store is that you can ask the employees questions that you might not be able to get answered online. There is the option of sending questions to the seller, but sometimes they either don't reply or don't understand the question. In store, you can also ask if people have returned the product, if they have tried it, and what others say about it. At the mall, you can also socialize and hang out with friends. Researching and buying things online happens mostly when you're by yourself, so it's nice to spend time with family and friends. You can also do your own research with friends by comparing prices between two different stores. This is something that I do a lot; when I want to see if another store has more options or better pricing, I will either ask the cashier to hold on to my item, or I'll hide it myself. The last thing that's great about buying in store is that you get a lot of exercise walking around!

Buying online also has a lot of benefits, like the convenience and speed in which you can buy things. You don't have to wait in line to scan items; maybe you have anxiety and don't want to interact with people; or maybe you just don't have the time it takes to travel to the mall, find parking, and then try and find your item by browsing different shops. Instead, you just go to Amazon, type in what you want to buy, look at the possible options and ratings, and then just click on *Buy*. If you have an account, then you don't even have to put in your address or payment information. The only problem with buying online is that you have to pay for shipping, someone might steal the box off your porch, the item might get damaged in shipping, and you have to wait for it to arrive. But it is easier and faster to research because you don't have to walk to different stores remembering the prices. In summary, buying in store and online have their own pros and cons, and you should do a mix of both to get the best of both worlds.

Research

Notes

Notes

Chapter 7

Track

Create a Budget (make sure to set realistic goals for how much you can spend per week)

The last letter of the acronym is **T**, which stands for tracking. Tracking consists of writing it down when you spend money. The first thing that you can do is create a budget. This means that you have to make realistic goals for how much money you spend each week. The problem is if you think you can go from spending $300 a week to $20 a week, you're obviously not being very realistic with yourself—unless you have amazing self-control, and can quit cold turkey. Not only that but you also need to include your expenses. As a teenager, you don't have as many expenses as when you're an adult.

I find that the easiest way to create a simple budget is to write it on paper. So to begin with, you would write down your expenses. For me, I would write down my bill for Crunchyroll ($7), my YouTube premium ($12), and my cell phone bill ($75). I would then write down how much I make for that month. So, I make about $700 a month. I then would have to remove the bills that I have, so when I add the expenses, it comes to $159. Then I have to deduct common needs like sanitary napkins, which costs $11.

So I have about $170 that I need to spend per month. After that, I decide that I want to cut down how much money I spend on going out once a week, which costs around $30 ($10 for food and $20 to spend in total). Then, $30x4 is $120, to spend on whatever you want. To make sure that you're saving up enough money, to find total income, subtract expenses and recreational money. So, $700-$170-$120 is $410 that you're saving up per month. The nice thing for us teens is that we don't have to subtract expenses for food, electricity bills, etc. Now, depending on how much you make, the amount of money you can spend changes. The amount you spend also depends on what type of person you are.

Let's say you're a guy who doesn't really like to go to the mall or spend money. Maybe instead of spending the $30 each week, you decide to save up the money to buy a pair of Nikes. Or maybe you like to go out a lot in a week, and go out 3 times a week, only spending enough to buy a basic lunch at $10. How you budget your money is up to you, and I really don't know what type of person reads this book. Something you can do is try different methods of saving and spending money until you find the one that best suits you.

Have a Physical Way of Tracking Money

This page is going to be aimed at those who are more likely to splurge. If you're someone who is more likely to spend money, then I suggest not going to places where you'd be more tempted to buy things. This means avoiding going to malls or department stores. Just like if someone is trying to quit drinking, you would not bring an alcoholic to a liquor store. Shopping compulsively or uncontrollably can be considered as an addiction to buying things.

Track

When you buy things, do you feel a rush, or feel really excited when buying something new, only to never use the item you bought. Maybe before you start saving money, you should track one month or one week of spending. Every time you spend money on anything, write it down. In the next page, I'll expand on the idea of analyzing that data. But right now, you should focus on how you should limit yourself. When you do go out that one time per week, make sure to go somewhere where you won't be tempted to spend all your money. Maybe you go to a rink where the only possible thing you can buy would be food or skate rentals. This is one of the best ways to prevent you from spending that money.

Another thing you can do when you go out is to only carry the amount of money you plan to spend. That way, you physically can't spend money you don't have. Another thing you can do to track how you're buying things would be to use physical money, because you can get a sense of how much you're spending. I personally find that I buy most of my things with my credit card. Part of the reason why I do this is because I want to take advantage of the cash back of 1% interest. Not only that, but each time I'm buying and then paying back the amount of money, I'm building my credit score. Every time I do buy, I always make sure that I have that amount of money available in my debit account.

When you do go out that one time per week, also make sure that you don't make it an excuse to spend all your money on that one day. You can do so by keeping to a budget. You can keep to this budget by either only carrying that amount of money, setting a reminder, or even making the amount part of your lock screen. You can even write it on a sticky note and attach it to your debit card. There are many ways to prevent you from splurging your money, but this doesn't mean that you will use them. It's up to you to decide whether you'll buy something or not.

Put Away a Certain Percentage of a Paycheck and Have a Certain Amount to Spend

The next way you can stick to your budget is by using separation. This might mean that each time you get a pay check, you decide on a percentage of the amount of money you do want to spend. Let's say you get paid $350 every two weeks and you know that you have expenses of $170 per month, or $85 per two weeks, you could divide 85 by 350 to see how much money you'd spend on expenses per paycheck, and this equals to around 25%. This means that for every paycheck you get, you spend 40% of that paycheck. This is a pretty good ratio of how much money you'll be spending and saving.

It's up to you as to what ratios you want to use. You could also just do 50% saving and 50% spending. Another thing you can do is separate your bank accounts so that you have one specifically for the money you're putting away. This would be the bank account that you can only deposit from, not withdraw. The next account would be the one holding the money that you are allowed to spend that week. This account would always be under $100 and would be taking money from your last account. This is the money that is the gray area, it's the amount that is available to spend or save. So once you get that paycheck, you would be putting $52 in the gray area bank account. Then, for the week, you would transfer $26 that you can either spend or save.

Let's say you don't spend all of the $26; it's up to you to either keep it in the spending bank account, put it into the savings account, or transfer it to the gray area for emergencies. This method does sound like it will take a lot of effort, but thanks to banking companies having apps, you can easily transfer the money between all three accounts in seconds. This method of three accounts is aimed at those who spend more money and can't control their spending habits. It's a more drastic method because if you go over the budget, it will decline your card. This can be an embarrassing experience, but it helps remind the person that they are over their budget, and it teaches them to keep better track of it. The only problem is if you are aware of the amount you have to spend on a big ticket item that you've been saving up for. This is why there is a simpler method where you just use two accounts. You would just put 40% (or whatever percentage you want), and the 60% into the saving account, which you can only deposit to. Another thing that you can do is to put the savings money in an account that builds interest. This way, the longer it stays in that account, the more money you get back for free.

How to Successfully Track Your Money

How do I efficiently track how much I'm spending and saving? I'd say that the easiest way you can start to track your money is to get a daily planner and write down on each date how much you spend and on what. Once you have this information, you can see if you're spending your money on things you actually need, or on things that you wanted. Once you have identified the problem that you have, you have to figure out how you will stop doing this.

Maybe you can create a step by step plan. An example of this would be if you noticed that you're spending over $70 on junk food, and that you need to figure out ways to reduce that amount. You might want to spend more money on buying healthy food, or put time in your day to create a healthy lunch that you can put into a container. This way, you won't feel the urge to buy junk food, because you will already have food that you have made to eat. Another thing you can do is avoid the places that have the junk food. Let's say there's a MacDonald's at the end of your street. To avoid even seeing the temptation, maybe you should take another route, go around the building, or even distract yourself with music.

Some of the possible positives of not buying the junk food would be saving money, maybe even losing some weight, and overall, helping your body stay healthy by eating healthier. Something that I noticed is that I spent a lot of money on cat toys and clothing for my kitten. After acknowledging that I spend too much on Felix, I realize that he doesn't really care because he's a cat; and not only that but sometimes he wouldn't play with the toys I bought him, and would rather play with a plastic bag. After acknowledging this, I now know that he has enough toys to be happy.

Therefore, when I see something that is either cute or that I might like, I think about whether I have the room for it, and that I do not need everything that I see. This way I can control my spending. If you track your spending all the time, including when you start to save money, you can always analyze the data that you create to better yourself. Also, you can look back at your old logs and think about how much you have changed.

Find Your Triggers

Because you have been tracking how much money you are spending, you start to learn what triggers you to buy something. Maybe you are drawn by the showcase of a store, or even just the name of your favourite store. Let's say that you figure out that you spend more money the day after you receive your paycheck. You should eliminate this temptation by avoiding malls the day after you get your paycheck, separating your money by using the 2 to 3 bank account system, or even avoiding shopping websites. You can't buy things if you don't know they exist. This means that you delete all the shopping apps on your phone, like eBay, Amazon, or Wish. You can even go as a far as blocking theses websites on your laptop.

Personally, I have deleted all my shopping apps. This meant deleting eBay, Amazon, and AliExpress. I found that this helped a lot because I tend to shop when I'm bored, as it causes me to become interested in something. An example of this might be if you're someone who spends a lot of money on makeup: you should avoid Sephora, unsubscribe from receiving newsletters, and maybe even avoid watching YouTubers who do makeup. This is because they usually list the products they use, or even release their own palettes. You can also inform your family that you're trying to avoid the things that you spend the most amount of money on. They might be able to catch you when you're tempted to buy something, and remind you of your budget.

I don't think you should be too hard on yourself if you do break budget, forget to write down an item, or forget to put away money in your savings account. The thing that is the most important is that you're putting your time and effort into becoming a better person. The only problem about having a physical calendar is if you lose the book or it gets ruined by water; then you are going to have a hard time analyzing the information that you have tracked. To prevent this, you could make one online by using an online calendar. You also wouldn't have to pay for paper or writing utensils. If you're a student at a high school, university, or college, they have Office 365 for free. This includes software like Word, Excel, OneNote, and PowerPoint. I personally use OneNote to keep track of all my school notes and to-do lists. You can use this software to keep track of your info. If you want something free, you can use software like Google Docs, where you can even share your files with others.

Use Technology to Your Advantage

The last way you can track things is by using technology to your advantage. There are a lot of apps to track how much you're spending. If you have a TD bank account like I do, they have an app that tracks your spending by using the information from your bank account. The nice thing about this is you don't have to provide the info of how much you're spending, because it already knows. An app that is really good for millennials is Wally. This app uses artificial intelligence to look at your data, analyze it, and provide feedback.

This is smarter than the TD app. The TD app only shows you how much you're spending and on what. So it categorizes it by transportation, food, and recreation. It also tells you what group you spend the most money on. If you do want to track your money by yourself, you can either use a calendar to track how much money you spend per day or you can create groups. These groups can be whatever you want. If you want it simple, you can just write wants or needs. If you want to be more specific, you could separate it into categories like food, recreation, travel, bills, clothing, or impulse buys. Every time that you'd buy something, you would then write the date and the amount of money that you spent. You could also use Excel spreadsheets if you're bad at doing math. You would put in the formula, like subtract cell a7 from a5. There are letters and numbers listed on both the y and x axis.

If you have taken a business class, then you should be familiar with Excel. If you want to find other money tracking apps, you can just google it, and there will be a lot of websites that can provide a list of apps that you can try out. Don't know how to use Excel, or want to try a different method of tracking? Look on YouTube: watch how others spend, make, analyze, research, and track their money. Something that you will notice in this book is that everything you need to do to save money are things for which you need to take the initiative. I may give you the idea of how to do something, or bring awareness to a possible issue, but it is totally up to you to follow my advice, modify it, ignore my advice, or find your own way to do it.

Notes

Track

Notes

Notes

Chapter 8

Avoid Temptations

Don't Bring a Wallet/Money

Congratulations! You have now read all about my SMART method. So, what are the next 3 chapters about? The next three chapters have even more advice, while Chapter 10 is a summary of the whole book! The first thing I will touch upon will be how to avoid temptations. The first tip I will give you is that you can avoid spending money by not having the money.

This means, when you are going out for a walk, you don't carry money, and this way, when you see something you want, you literally can't buy it. Another way to avoid temptations is to only bring the money you know you need. This might mean if you want to hang out with friends but still want to stick to your budget, you can bring $20 for food. This way, once that money is done, you can't buy anything. You also won't want to carry around any debit or credit cards. I find that this method actually also applies to adults as well.

This is because, when they go to a casino, it's really easy to spend all your money. If you, as an adult, only bring $50, once you have used that $50, no matter if you won more money or lost it all, it means it's time to go. It might not be as popular as it used to be, but you should only bring a certain amount of money to an arcade. They try and fool you by not using actual money to play games. Instead, you have to convert your money to coins and then use a certain amount of coins to play. This is something that a lot of games do, including mobile games. You might have to pay $5 to buy 50 gems. This way, it seems like you're unable to keep track of how much money you're spending.

When I was a little girl, I would go to Great Wolf Lodge for the winter break, with my sister and dad. When we went to the arcade, Dad would just give us $40 each to get a certain amount of tokens. He would then say that once those tokens were used up, then that means we were done playing. This amount of money would last a good one to two hours. We would then go and have a machine count our tickets, and then look at the prizes. I think the arcade system has been updated and uses cards for tokens, and also for the tickets, which makes it easier because you don't have to count the amount of tickets you have. (This was part of the fun though.) But much like a debit card, you don't know how many more tokens you have left until it's all gone.

Delete Shopping Apps

Something that I personally find myself doing, when I'm bored, is browsing on shopping websites. Even when I don't want to buy anything specific, I might find myself buying something because I learnt about it after browsing. This is why I suggest you delete any shopping apps you have, and this may include Amazon, eBay, Wish, or AliExpress. You can even go as far as blocking the actual websites. If I don't have the apps to browse, I can't buy the products.

Avoid Temptations

These shopping apps are specifically made to catch your attention, especially Wish. Wish always has low prices and shipping. Some items are labelled as free, and you only need to pay for shipping. This doesn't mean that the item is free; it means that it costs as much as the shipping, with free shipping. This method of marketing makes it seem like you're getting a good deal while actually making profit. I had this happen to me when I saw an ad for a free Tamagotchi. I only had to pay shipping. The shipping cost $5, and it took more than 2 months to appear. Once I received the item, I could tell that it was really bad quality.

Because I was curious as to how much it retailed for, I googled the model and found out it costs $2 online. That means that the seller made a profit of $3 per item. Not only that, but I bet a lot of people bought that item because it was *free*. Because this happened to me, I wanted to share my experience so it doesn't happen to you. The problem with apps like AliExpress and Wish, where the price is $3 instead of $12, is the shipping. This is because they are usually shipping from China, using the cheapest method of shipping, which takes 2–3 months to arrive at your door. If you really need to buy something online, I would recommend Amazon. Not only does it have one to two-day shipping, and free returns, the return process of Amazon is one of the big reasons I shop there. If you don't want or like an item, or it's broken, you can print out a return label and use the packaging it came in to return it. It's also a lot more reliable than other websites, because they expect you to pay for your own shipping, and getting in contact with the seller is more challenging.

Remove Apple or Android Pay

Nowadays, a lot of young adults use their devices to pay, thanks to services like Apple pay, Google Pay, or Android Pay. I personally use Apple Pay a lot. This is due to the fact that I usually have my iPhone in my hand, so I don't need to go through my purse trying to find my wallet and then my debit card. Instead, I just put my finger on the home button, and it then automatically opens up Apple Pay, and I tap my device to the card reader. The problem with paying with your devices is how much faster and efficient it is to pay. If you have to take the extra steps it takes to get your debit card or cash out, it gives you the time to reflect if you really need the item you're buying.

Also, you might not be keeping track of what you're buying when using Apple Pay because it has even less steps than using a debit card. This is because it can become second nature just to use tap and leave, not thinking about how much you're spending. Something you can do to help spend less money may be increasing how much you can spend on tap. It defaults to $100 as the max amount, but you could change this to $50, or even $20 at a time. This way if you go over the max amount, your tap won't work.

Another thing about Apple Pay, which is both convenient and a problem when you're trying to budget, would be that you always have your phone on you. I've had times where I forget to bring my wallet but I can pay with Apple Pay. This means that you'd always have a way to spend money; so if you do limit how much money you have on you, you still have Apple Pay, which you could use. This is why I suggest, if you are someone who is more likely to impulse buy or have less self-control, you should remove Apple Pay. I remember that I removed Apple Pay for 2 weeks, and I noticed just how much I rely on it. I would open the wallet app, only to see that I had no cards, which means that sometimes I just had to leave without buying anything, because I forgot my wallet.

Remind Yourself of Your Budget

The next thing you should do when you're on a budget is to create reminders. Maybe when you go to the mall, you create a temporary background with the amount of money you can spend that day. Another thing you could do is create an alarm for when you actually are about to meet up with a friend or get to your location. Some teenagers don't have the luxury of owning or driving a car. Personally, I use public transit to get around.

So, I'd open google maps, type in the location, and it would give me an approximate time that I'd arrive at the mall. Let's say you leave at 3 pm, and it says you will arrive at 3:45. You can just ask Siri to set an alarm, labelled *max spend $20 for 3:45*. This way, right when you get excited to be at the mall, sometimes even overwhelmed, you have that alarm to remind you of your objective. Another thing you can do is add a sticky note to your debit card or on your bills. This way, right when you're about to buy something, you're immediately reminded of how much you are allowed to spend, right when you're about to spend. The last way you can remind yourself, which is a bit more drastic, is to set limits on your debit or visa card, or even put a certain amount of money in one bank account. This way, if you go over your budget, then your card will decline.

This will be an embarrassing experience, but it serves as a hard reminder and lesson on what happens when you don't keep track of your budget or you go over it. I personally have never had my card declined, but I had a friend whose card declined because he didn't put enough funds in his spending account. This makes it seem like you don't have enough money, which will become reality if you don't learn to control your spending. I have bought on impulse, and when this happened, I didn't think about my budget at all.

Sometimes I've had times where I have spent over the budget, so I just say screw it and buy even more things that day. Something you can do to combat this is to keep the receipts of the things you have bought, and not to open the packaging immediately. When I bought a makeup palette that cost me $30, I kept the receipt, thought about it, and returned it the next day. This is how you can recover from an impulse buy.

Identify Good Sales and Ignore Bad Ones

Another way to avoid temptation is to avoid sales. Sometimes I reason buying an item because it's on sale. But there are some sales that are used as door busters, and this means they are only there to draw customers in to buy even more. An example of a bad sale would be the bogo sale. Bogo used to mean *buy one get one free*, but nowadays it seems to be more of *buy one get one 50% off*. Now, if we analyze this sale, we can see that you're really only getting 25% off each item, which isn't that good. If it was an actual *bogo*, where you save 50% on each item, it would be a better deal. The problem is, sometimes you only need one item, not two, and the bogo forces you to buy two items, which is just more clutter.

Avoid Temptations

Sometimes a store always has sales to create the illusion that you need to buy that item today or it will be full price, but in reality, it's always on sale. This would be the case at Urban Planet. I bet they just raise the retail prices on the tags; so you're actually just paying the normal price for the item when it's on sale, because the retail price is just inflated. A good rule to go by, if you only save $5 or less, is that the item does not have a good sale, so you shouldn't buy it. Sales start to get good once it crosses 50% markdowns. The best type of sale is when they have an extra markdown on already marked down items. This way of shopping means you're paying $3 for a decent quality shirt.

Another place that has great sales is Value Village. Twice a year, they have 50% off their clothing, which is already cheaper than buying new clothes. There are also places like Winners and Homesense, which give out the suggested retail price, and then give their own price. The problem with this is that it has been shown to not be the actual retail price. Therefore, when I shop there, I also check online to make sure that I'm actually saving money buying there. This type of store is also the type that only has a few copies of a product, and sometimes there is only one available.

This is the type of store where it is better to buy it before someone else gets it. The good thing about Homesense, Winners, and TJ Maxx is that they have a really good return policy. This way, you can reflect overnight if you really need and want the item, and as long as you don't take it out of the packaging, they will accept the return. You should make sure to tape the receipt to the product so you don't lose it.

Don't Browse, As You Will Buy!
When you buy, have a list! Stick to it.

The last way to avoid temptations is to *stick to it*. A lot of stores, like Target or IKEA, put the basic items at the end of the hall. This way you have to walk all around the store, trying to find the items on your list. By the time you get to the needed item, you have a full cart. Sometimes people even forget what they came for and return home with items they never needed. You can beat the system by keeping a list of what you need. I suggest either writing on a piece of paper and using a pen to cross off items, or texting yourself a list, if you'd rather use technology. Now, this method of sticking only to your list really depends if you're able to avoid temptation, so it really tests your self-control.

Also, make sure not to browse when you're shopping. If you go browsing with the thought that you won't buy anything, you'll end up buying things. As already mentioned, if you can't see it, you can't buy it. If you have enough self-control to browse, make sure that you either don't have money on you or remind yourself of your budget. When my mom and I go shopping at Costco, we make a list of the things we need. When I was there, there were a lot of things you could check out, but that doesn't mean you have to buy them. Just like anyone else, we aren't perfect; we bought things that weren't on our list. It mostly consisted of other food we didn't think of, like bananas and something for supper. This is an example of how we are just human, so if you do buy something while browsing, it's okay—as long as it doesn't become a common occurrence, and you learn from it.

When we were at Costco, it was when there were sample stations everywhere! We did try a lot of samples, and since it's free, it's

Avoid Temptations

okay. But we didn't buy anything from the sampling stations. We usually just have the samples for little snacks. Another thing that is common at Costco and other stores would be in-store demos. This is when there is someone there who shows you how to use a product, and you can ask questions. Not only that but they usually have testimonials from customers. My mom has bought something from a demo; it was a $200 cream. I tried it because it claimed to help people with eczema, but it actually made it worse. I find that demos are obviously there to put the product in a positive light, and it's up to you if you want to buy it or not. Just know, if it sounds too good to be true, it usually is.

Notes

Avoid Temptations

Notes

Notes

Chapter 9

Cheap or Free Ways to Have Fun

Community Centres

Now that I have given you ways to make money, what are some ways you can have a good time, either by yourself or with friends, with either no cost or a low price. The first way to have fun for a small fee would be by going to a community centre. In Mississauga, community centres have fun swim days, where you pay $3 if you're under 18, and $3.75 if you're older than 17. This is a great way to have fun with friends when you have a budget, and not only that, but you would be getting a workout.

Whenever my friends and I go swimming, we play games like tag, go on the slide, and just chill in the hot tub and catch up on life. Another activity you can do at community centres would be skating. If you live in Mississauga, then you should know that there is a free skating rink across from Square One Mall. It's really nice at night because they always have beautiful Christmas lights. If you don't like skating outside, there are some community centres that have indoor skating rinks. In the winter time, they have free skating on certain dates, thanks to Tim Hortons. You would have to bring your own pair of skates though, but don't worry if you don't have any; you can rent some for $10. If you tend to skate often, I would recommend buying a pair of skates because it would save you more money in the long run. Community centres also have drop-in programs, like drop-in boot camp, which is where you work out, have tai chi in the water, and lots more.

You can get a full list of these activities if you google *community centre drop-in schedule at "your city."* Something that saves you even more money (if you live in Mississauga), if you're 12–14 years old, is something called a freedom pass. You can go to a community centre to apply and get one. It's a pass that allows you to swim for free, in both indoor and outdoor pools, and it is also for free transit in Mississauga. It starts July 1st and ends August 31st. If you're a teenager who is older than 14, you should have a Presto pass. A Presto pass saves you money when paying for transit. Instead of paying $3.75, you're paying $2.25. If you take transit every single day, then it's a good idea to get a monthly pass. Public transit is a cheaper alternative to using an uber or a taxi. It may take a bit longer, but it's worth using it for the price.

Library

A library is a great place to go when you have spare time. A lot of people think that libraries are boring. I am someone who still reads physical books every now and then. The Mississauga library makes it easy to put certain titles on hold. Sometimes there is a waiting list, but that's usually for the main stream books. The library has a new program that lets you rent out eBooks by using an app on your phone, called Overdrive. Thanks to this system, you don't have to wait on a list to receive the book or travel to the library to pick it up. As long as you return your books and material on time, there is no fee for using the library.

Something that may interest you more about the library is that you can actually borrow video games and movies.

These have a shorter borrowing period of about a week, versus 3 weeks. This is a good way to either play with yourself or friends, without spending any money. I recommend borrowing video games that don't have a storyline, unless you can beat the game in that one week. This is because there is only one saved file on a game, and everyone will be using this file. This means that any progress you make will be lost once you return it. You could play games like Mario Kart or Super Smash Bros., but if you really want to play games like Legend of Zelda, go ahead. You can easily see what you have checked out or have on hold on their website, or you can be notified via text when you have a hold that has arrived, or an overdue item. The library is also a great place to study for exams or do assignments.

They have specifically built quiet rooms and areas so people can work without being disturbed. These are the areas where the rule of being quiet is emphasized. I tend to use this quiet space a lot because it gets me into work mode without being distracted by noise or my device. The last amazing thing that libraries have is computers and free Wi-Fi. Did your Wi-Fi at home stop working, or do you need to type up an essay, but your mom is using your laptop? You can book a computer online, and it has a one hour limit. But it can go over this limit if no one has booked the computer you are on. You can also just drop in and see if there are any computers available. The Wi-Fi also means, if you bring your own computer in, you can connect to the internet.

Fairs and Festivals

The next way you can have fun while saving money would be by going to a fair or a festival. In Mississauga, there are always a lot of festivals or events, like Ribfest, the Santa Claus Parade, or BuskerFest. These events have free admission, and you can buy things like carnival food or novelty items, but that's up to you. At the festivals, they have live singers who you can listen to and watch for free. Whenever there is a festival in my area, I always tend to visit it. One time, they even had a cheese festival, where they gave out free samples of cheese. Sometimes I spend money at these festivals, especially when I'm with friends. I usually spend that money on food. The food there is usually under $10 per item, so it would stay within your budget. Some festivals even have rides. Recently, I went to the Christmas Market in Toronto, and they had a Ferris wheel and carousel, which cost $5 per ride.

If you go to a festival, make sure to avoid the carnival games. These games have the goal of getting the most money out of you as possible. Some people get fixated on a plushie that you can buy online for much cheaper than what it costs to play for it. Not only that but you have to actually win the game. Some vendors even go as far as rigging the game—maybe they put weights in a jar so it doesn't knock over—either way, you wouldn't know. A public event that a lot of people go to see is the Santa Claus Parade. These parades usually have really cool floats and even free samples. I recommend that you bring a set amount of money when going to any public event. This is because they will try and grab your attention, and try to get you to spend money. I remember there used to be a fair in North Bay where my grandma lived, and when I was a little kid, I would go there.

Cheap or Free Ways to Have Fun

Even when I was little, I avoided the games that had prizes. Instead, I went on rides like the huge slide that you use a bag to slide down on. The next events that are free are fireworks or air shows. You can see a lot of fireworks on any holiday, but the big ones would be New Years and Canada Day. It's always a fun experience seeing them fly in the air and explode whilst making a lot of noise. Another thing that you can watch is canoe racing. In Port credit, around the summer time, there is a day where they have canoe racing all day. It is entertaining to watch, especially when the ducks swim near them.

Volunteer

The next way to have fun can also help your community. Volunteering is when you give up your time and effort to an event, program, or foundation, without being paid. I used to volunteer for Erin Oak Kids. This is a foundation that helped support families that had kids who had disabilities. This could range from autism to cerebral palsy. I volunteered for a drama program, where I gained a lot of knowledge and had fun new experiences and bonds with the children. If you're in high school, then you know you have a minimum of 40 hours of volunteering. I think you should try volunteering not just because you have to but because you want to gain new skills and experiences whilst helping others. You can even volunteer for a fundraiser, where you raise money for a cause. My friend volunteers for a skating event, and the money goes to help people in need.

I remember when my high school class volunteered at a local shelter, where we fed the homeless. That was an experience that definitely changed my outlook on life, and I realized how grateful I am for my current financial situation. That experience really humbled me. If you're afraid to volunteer by yourself, volunteer with a friend. This way, you can learn new things, and do something without knowing ahead of time what you may learn, with someone you're familiar with. This can also make time fly by if things are slow. Volunteering can range from a one-day event that lasts 6 hours, to a 4-month program where you're there 3 hours a day, once a week— it's really up to you what you want to do. Once you've volunteered for a certain event, you might want to do so the following year! I suggest volunteering when you're under 16 years old. This is because, once you get in your higher teens, you should be looking for paid work.

I personally stopped volunteering after grade 10 ended, and I looked for a job until I got one in November of my 11th year at school. This is due to the fact that you should start making an income so you have more financial freedom. The process to volunteering can either be very long or short. Sometimes you just have to fill out a form, giving basic facts, like name, age, and address; while on other forms, you have to give a reason why you should be allowed to volunteer, and sometimes you are even asked for a background check. The more thorough interviews, for a volunteer position, usually happen for more in-demand roles, or for working with children. I can't even imagine trying to volunteer for the Olympic Games, as I'm guessing that would take a lot of screening!

Learn Something New

The next thing you can do to entertain yourself is to learn something new. This could mean that you look online to find instructions on how to do something. Depending on what you're learning to do, the time it takes to learn varies. You could learn something as simple as how to whistle, or how to play the recorder. This way, you can improve yourself by gaining new knowledge. Another way to learn something new is to either watch fact videos or read about facts. Let's say you want to learn how to play an instrument. If you're on a budget, you're obviously not going to go out and buy a $400 flute. No; instead, you can go to the dollar store and pick up a recorder. This was actually what I was supposed to learn in grade 4, but then my music teacher passed away, and I ended up having a supply teacher the rest of the year.

After buying the recorder, you can watch videos on how to read sheet music, and how to hold a recorder properly. Something that I think teenagers should try learning is knitting. Knitting is something that has a really small investment: you pay for the yarn and needles. The nice thing is, once you get the basic technique down, you can knit almost anything. My sister learnt knitting from my grandma, and she made hats, scarves, and gloves. You could even make a business out of knitting items. My sister recently learnt how to play guitar, thanks to the internet. This is something that takes a lot of discipline, because you have to be able to set aside time to learn, and then practise what you learnt. Also, if you don't understand something or are having trouble, there isn't a real person to help you. You could ask online, but then someone has to be both competent in the subject and nice enough to give you a hand. I find that if you learn how to do something that can create an item, then that really shows a physical example of how you learnt something new. This can also fulfill a personal goal, doing something you've always wanted to. Another low cost thing to learn is how to do origami, or how to solve a Rubik's cube. There are so many things to do, and it's only limited by your imagination and willingness to learn. You could even do something as simple as learning how to cook. This is not only a cheaper alternative to buying fast food, but it's also healthier—you know what you're putting in your body because you cooked it.

Play Outside, Hang Out With Friends

Another way you can have fun is by hanging out with friends. The nice thing about hanging out with friends is that it can make even the most tedious task, like cleaning your room, fun. People think that you always spend money when hanging out with friends, but there are ways for you to have fun with friends without spending money. The first one is by hanging out at someone's house. When you hang out at someone's house, there are a lot of things you can do. You can play video games, board games, or card games. This is a fun way to interact with one another. If my friends come to my house, I have a Wii gaming console (This is pretty old, but I rarely play games nowadays.). The next great thing about hanging out at someone's house is that you're less likely to buy food at a restaurant.

This is because most people have food in their house. I tend to find, when people come to my house, that we can cook some badass and delicious tasting food. I personally like to cook thick udon noodles, with eggs, bacon, and mushrooms, while using Asian sauces like rice vinegar. Another thing you can do together is something more challenging, like building Ikea furniture—maybe you have a project that you want to work on, and your friend's cool with helping you. Personally, I wanted to get around to adding a marble vinyl to my desk, because it looks cute and goes well with the room. You can even go outside and play games like soccer or tag. Tag may seem like a juvenile game to play, but trust me when I say it never gets old.

Something my friends and I do a lot is walk to a park and swing on the swings. This activity is free, and it makes you go outside and absorb some vitamin D. If you want to watch a movie, you can find them free on YouTube, or you can use Netflix if you have an account. You can even rent a DVD from the YouTube store for $5, or borrow it from the library for free. I personally have been using the YouTube library because it's a fast way to get HD quality without having to deal with ads, or risk the chance of viruses. If you don't have a DVD player, which a lot of teens don't, YouTube has millions of videos you can entertain yourself with.

Notes

Cheap or Free Ways to Have Fun

Notes

Notes

Chapter 10

What You Can Do To Be Financially Successful

Follow the SMART Model

Now that you have read all about my methods and my ways to save money, I'm going to give you some final tips on how to maintain good habits and be successful. To begin with, the first thing you need to do is follow the SMART model. This means *saving* money by creating a budget so you are aware of how much you can spend on both your wants and needs, and by going the extra mile to save money by finding coupons, going to thrift stores, or getting an item on sale. I personally save a lot of money by going to Value Village for my clothing, or by buying things on sale. Another thing that I like to use for saving money is the percentage technique: keeping 60% of my paycheck for savings, and being able to spend the rest. A good way to *make money* could mean finding a part time job, or even starting your own business. I actually made a bookmark company when I was 10 years old. I had a business partner, and we made about $50 in profits.

This was actually part of a business camp, where I had a lot of fun! If your parents are overprotective, or you're unable to get a part time job, you can always do chores around the house. *Analyze* is the next technique, and this means you take that extra pause to think before you buy. Sometimes you might even have to sleep on it before buying an item. You can also analyze the value of an item and if it's worth the time and effort it took for you to make the money you're about to spend.

Next up is *research*, and this means comparing prices online and seeing which retailer has the better deal. You might even find a better deal online! The last letter stands for *track*, and this means using a system to record every time you spend money. From this, you can become aware of how much you're spending and what may trigger you to buy. Thanks to tracking what you spend the most money on, you can prevent it from happening again.

Be Responsible

To begin with, what does responsible mean? Responsibility is when you become the cause of something—you'll either be blamed or credited for this action. This is something that you have already started to do. You're taking the initiative to read this book and to better yourself. It's going to be up to you to regulate your spending. For some of you, this will be the hardest part of saving money: having the willpower to not spend all your money. Responsibility will be part of your whole life. You're responsible for your actions, so if you punch someone, then expect to face the repercussions. This also applies to personal finance: Did you spend $200 on a pair of shoes you didn't need?

Guess what? You have not only gone over your budget, but you also now have debt on your credit card, because you were not paying attention to how much money you have. At the same time, if you make a mistake, it's okay—if you learn from it and never do it again. But if you make a mistake and never acknowledge or review why you have problems after, then you'll be stuck in an endless cycle of never having enough money. I find that the older I get, the more responsibilities I seem to have. Personally, as I've gotten older, the more bills I have to pay.

Once you turn 18 years old, you're not considered a minor anymore, and this means you can be charged with criminal offenses. You are also able to get a credit card. I find that it's actually better for your parents to keep you accountable for your actions, so that you learn what happens when you don't obey the law. If you're never taught responsibility as a child, and how, if you break a toy, you don't just get a new one, then you'll be pretty shocked when things start to get out of hand because you're not responsible enough to control your actions.

A good example of someone not being responsible would be some people on YouTube who lose their temper and either trash the store, swear a lot, or get into an altercation. This usually ends up with them getting arrested. Anyway, once you learn to be responsible for your actions, you'll be able to control what you're buying, because you would have analyzed whether an item's value is worth its price. Being financially smart means that you think about how to spend your money by paying attention to your budget and sticking to it.

Start Investing Money ASAP

This is something that the earlier you start the better. When you invest your own money into something, there will be a percentage of interest, which you get back each month. This means that the more money you have saved up, the more money you're going to get. Wouldn't you rather start saving at age 18, than at 30? There are multiple ways to invest money as a teen. You usually have to wait until you're 18 years old, because that is when you can buy stocks. There are websites like Stockpile or Stash. These websites make it easier for young adults to start investing money. Stocks are a percentage of the company that is sold off to potential buyers. A bond is a contract between two people; it's also considered debt. The stock market is where people's stocks and bonds are bought and sold. I personally haven't started investing money in the stock market, so I don't have much experience. I just know that investing in stocks can be somewhat of a tricky business.

This is because the stocks are always fluctuating in price. Something that I would recommend, if you have at least $10,000, would be to invest in real estate. As a teenager, this is a less viable option, as most teens don't have that type of money; they just know that houses always go up in value, while cars go down in value, the minute they are driven off the lot. If you're not comfortable with dealing with investment right now, then it's important to focus on saving as much money as you can while you don't have to pay for tons of bills and taxes. If you save at least 50% of your paycheck, then you should be pretty well off by the time you turn 20, depending on when you start. The good news is that you're already ahead of your friends by reading this book.

Personally, I have been saving up money since I was around 5 or 6, but that is due to the fact that my mom made me financially aware at a young age. I think the most important thing to teach your future children (if you have any) is how to deal with money.

Let's say your parents are encouraging you to be financially literate, and maybe they even bought you this book in hopes that you will be more successful than them at saving money. You should be grateful that your parents care about your future. For some of you, your parents might be totally against you learning about money. I know my grandparents were. Because of this, you have to take the initiative to start investing or saving your money as soon as possible. As they say, money is what drives the world, but it's not what brings happiness.

Use Technology to Your Advantage

The next thing you need to remember is how much technology can help you. In finance, you can use programs like Excel, where you can learn to make spreadsheets and tables of your budget by using math equations. Another way to use technology would be by tracking your daily budget. Some banks even have an app that tracks how much you spend by linking to your bank account. This really comes in handy because you don't have to put in the info; and not only that, it classifies purchases by categories, like travel, recreation, or food. Something that is great about technology is that you can have a whole bunch of information stored on one small device. There are apps where you can even use your phone to scan the barcode on an item, and then be told how much the item should be sold for, the item's info, including the ranking, and even the reviews.

Another thing you can use your phone for is to compare prices. Let's say you're looking at buying the Nintendo Switch, but you want the best deals. Well, you can use a website like Google Shopping. I personally have used this website to compare prices for a Nintendo 2DS Pikachu Edition. I ended up getting the best deal on Amazon for $275, which is $75 more expensive than the base model. This is because you're paying for the limited edition. The nice thing about using technology is that you usually have your device on you at all times, so it's more convenient than using paper. There is also a smaller chance of losing your phone versus losing the paper. You can use a program like OneNote, which updates via Wi-Fi, and you can use it on your laptop, or any devices that support the app, like a tablet or phone.

Personally, I use this almost every day in school. This is because it's an easy way to stay organized. There are programs, like a calendar button or a to-do list, and it loads to all your devices. Not only that, but it's easy to read because it's typed up (I have really messy handwriting so I always type my work.).

Create Your Own Wealth

If you want to be successful, you need to find a source of income. Getting a part time job means that you have less control of what you do: A boss tells you what to do, and you have no say. This also means you can't pick the hours you have to work. Sometimes you won't be able to request a day off, and your schedule is always based around what days you work. The nice thing about having a part time job, like being a cashier, is that once your shift is over, you don't have to bring work home. This is definitely not the case if you start your own business. As a teenager, you don't have much money to start a business, but if you have an idea, you can always try and invent it.

There are websites, like Indiegogo, that help small entrepreneurs to get funding for great ideas. I have supported people on Indiegogo, and I'm always pleased with the items I have purchased. Let's say you're good at making necklaces. You could make an account on Etsy, and start setting time aside in your day to create some necklaces. You could create a certain amount of styles, or custom made necklaces that are made to order. This way, you won't have losses because you'd only be buying the materials when someone has ordered one. The problem with owning your own business is that you never leave the work at work. You work from home, and it will take up the majority of your time because you'll always have to manage it.

Something that is good about owning your own business is that you're your own boss. This means you can create your own work hours, but sometimes having too much freedom can be detrimental. I remember having a part time job where I was my own boss. I had to spend time calling people, booking demos, and then traveling to the demo, but I was only being paid for the one hour of the demo. This took a lot of energy because I had to spend a lot of time out of work trying to book appointments, practising my demo, and traveling to the client. I am grateful for this experience because I did learn a lot. One last way you can create wealth for yourself would be by doing tasks for people you know. This might mean cleaning your room or vacuuming the carpet to earn some change. You can even ask your neighbour's if they want their grass cut for $5. There is no limit to how many ways you can make cash—the only limit is your imagination.

Have a Positive Attitude

The final piece of advice I can give you is to be positive. This doesn't mean that you're not being realistic. If you mess up your budget, keep reminding yourself that you're human and make mistakes. Whenever you have a negative situation, think about a way that you can turn it into a positive. Let's say you have lost $20. Think about the possible opportunities or positives. You could hope that the money you dropped was found by someone who really needed the money for essentials, like food. If you only think about the negatives in life, it won't motivate you to do better.

Thinking negatively can actually result in you being depressed and not productive. You should also consider the people you hang around with. Is there anyone who you consider a friend, but they always call you fat and ugly? If a *friend* always insults you and makes you feel like crap, they're not your friend. There is a saying that who you hang out with reflects who you are. If you hang out with really rude people, who will never be successful in life, this will eventually influence you to be negative as well. I think being positive has to do with perseverance. Let's say you start your own company, and a thief steals $100 of your profit. You could be annoyed and devastated that your hard work wasn't rewarded; but you move on by working even harder, and maybe investing in a safe. If you just decided to give up because one person ruined your day, then you might have missed a possible opportunity.

Maybe a local news station picked up your story and brought attention to your product; thus making you even more sales than the amount that was stolen. If you had given up on your business, you would have got interviewed on the news, only to apologize that you have stopped making the product. In summary, I think it's important to have a positive outlook on life because you can enjoy and celebrate the mishaps and events you experience. Not only that, but you will be a lot more productive when you're thinking positively. If you find you're having difficulty with being successful and sticking to the SMART method, then you can make personal goals. Start small, and then go big! For example, for this book, I made small goals of finishing half a chapter. I celebrated every chapter I finished, as well as when I finished half the book, and finally, when I finished this chapter! Thanks to this way of setting goals, I was able to finish writing these ten chapters in 7 days!

Notes

Notes

Notes

About the Author

My name is Elizabeth. I was originally born in China and was adopted when I was a year old. My family consists of my mom, sister, and grandma. My father and grandpa passed away when I was 10 years old. I have faced many challenges in my life, including dealing with being legally blind in my left eye, having central auditory processing disorder, and a math/reading comprehension learning disability, which I learnt about in my senior year of high school. I also have severe food allergies, which makes going out to eat difficult. These are the negatives of my life that I have decided to embrace and turn into something positive. Since I was little, I have had a passion for reading books. When I was in grade 5, I was nominated to be the most likely to write a book, and I'm proud to have made this dream a reality. I learnt a lot about personal finance from a young age, thanks to my mom.

I am one of the youngest people to publish a book under the 10-10-10 program, and have just started my professional career. I am currently in Humber College for Business Administration Co-op. I hope this book can help expand your knowledge on how to save and spend your money wisely. Maybe your parents have bought this book for you, or maybe you discovered it on your own. Either way, I am proud that you have read this book, as you're taking a step towards adulthood.

Even though I have faced a lot of challenges in life, I try to keep a positive outlook, and I am determined to move toward my goal. I think it's important for teens to learn skills that will actually help them in life; like how to manage your money versus how to balance an equation. I hope you enjoy this book as much as I have enjoyed writing it. The info you gain from this book is priceless.

www.ingramcontent.com/pod-product-compliance
Lightning Source LLC
LaVergne TN
LVHW051501070426
835507LV00022B/2874